UNDERSTANDING

HUBERT SELBY, JR.

Understanding Contemporary American Literature
Matthew J. Bruccoli, Series Editor

Volumes on

Edward Albee • John Barth • Donald Barthelme
The Beats • The Black Mountain Poets
Robert Bly • Raymond Carver
Chicano Literature • Contemporary American Drama
Contemporary American Horror Fiction
Contemporary American Literary Theory
Contemporary American Science Fiction
James Dickey • E. L. Doctorow • John Gardner
George Garrett • John Hawkes • Joseph Heller
John Irving • Randall Jarrell • William Kennedy
Ursula K. Le Guin • Denise Levertov • Bernard Malamud
Carson McCullers • Arthur Miller • Toni Morrison's Fiction
Vladimir Nabokov • Joyce Carol Oates • Tim O'Brien
Flannery O'Connor • Cynthia Ozick • Walker Percy
Katherine Anne Porter • Reynolds Price • Thomas Pynchon
Theodore Roethke • Philip Roth • Hubert Selby, Jr.
Mary Lee Settle • Isaac Bashevis Singer • Gary Snyder
William Stafford • Anne Tyler • Kurt Vonnegut
Tennessee Williams

UNDERSTANDING
HUBERT
SELBY, JR.

JAMES R. GILES

University of South Carolina Press

© 1998 University of South Carolina

Published in Columbia, South Carolina, by the
University of South Carolina Press

Manufactured in the United States of America

02 01 00 99 98   5 4 3 2 1

Library of Congress Cataloging-in-Publication Data

Giles, James Richard, 1937-
    Understanding Hubert Selby, Jr. / James R. Giles.
        p.   cm. — (Understanding contemporary American
literature)
    Includes bibliographical references and index.
    ISBN 1–57003–176–2
    1. Selby, Hubert—Criticism and interpretation.   I. Title.
II. Series.
PS3569.E547Z68 1998
813'.54—dc21   97–4721

*To Wanda
and
to my graduate students in the Department of English
at Northern Illinois University who have helped me
to understand contemporary American literature*

CONTENTS

EDITOR'S PREFACE

The volumes of *Understanding Contemporary American Literature* have been planned as guides or companions for students as well as good nonacademic readers. The editor and publisher perceive a need for these volumes because much of the influential contemporary literature makes special demands. Uninitiated readers encounter difficulty in approaching works that depart from the traditional forms and techniques of prose and poetry. Literature relies on conventions, but the conventions keep evolving; new writers form their own conventions—which in time may become familiar. Put simply, *UCAL* provides instruction in how to read certain contemporary writers—identifying and explicating their material, themes, use of language, point of view, structures, symbolism, and responses to experience.

The word *understanding* in the titles was deliberately chosen. Many willing readers lack an adequate understanding of how contemporary literature works; that is, what the author is attempting to express and the means by which it is conveyed. Although the criticism and analysis in the series have been aimed at a level of general accessibility, these introductory volumes are meant to be applied in conjunction with the works they cover. They do not provide a substitute for the works and authors they introduce, but rather prepare the reader for more profitable literary experiences.

M. J. B.

ACKNOWLEDGMENTS

As with all I write, this book would not have been possible without the help and encouragement of Wanda Giles, Karen Blaser, and the staff of the Interlibrary Loan Department in Founders Memorial Library at Northern Illinois University. In addition, my chair James I. Miller, Jr., has made availabe to me the technical support necessary to write it. James Mellard, Matt Bruccoli, and Bill Adams, my editor at the University of South Carolina Press, also provided invaluable encouragement and support. Finally, "Cubby" Selby, the subject of the book, has been a generous source of information and insight throughout its composition.

UNDERSTANDING

HUBERT SELBY, JR.

CHAPTER ONE

Understanding Hubert Selby, Jr.

Career

It would be an understatement to say that Hubert Selby made a dramatic entrance into American literature. His first novel, *Last Exit to Brooklyn,* published by Grove Press in 1964, was clearly intended to shock and outrage readers and to challenge the conventions of decorum, restraint, and affirmative humanism on which American fiction had since the nineteenth century been based. Like the works of such other Grove Press writers of the 1950s and 1960s as William Burroughs and John Rechy, it explored subject matter that had traditionally been condemned and largely ignored in the accepted canon of the American novel. Its three central characters are a proud if doomed drag queen, an exploited and in turn rapacious prostitute, and a selfish and defiantly incompetent factory worker whose homosexual desires are becoming ever more urgent, more frightening, and thus more threatening. Episodic in narrative structure, *Last Exit to Brooklyn* derives its essential and subtle unity in part from the composite character of a roving Brooklyn street gang, the members of which strike out against the futility and boredom of their lives in acts of random brutality and savagery.

As if the depiction of such characters would not in itself be disturbing, the novel's mood reflects the rage of its creator. Seventeen years after its publication, Selby said in an interview with John O'Brien that, while writing it—as well as his next novel, *The Room* (1971)—he felt a deep "hatred for God" as a result of the pain, alienation, and near death he had experienced as a teenager.[1] The reader senses such authorial rage in *Last Exit to Brooklyn;* its narrative voice seems obsessed with denying even the slightest degree of hope and affirmation for the powerless and embittered figures who inhabit the grim and brutal world of Selby's novel.

In a recent letter to this writer Selby emphasized that his feelings toward God during this period were considerably more complex than the O'Brien interview would suggest:

> By the time I started THE ROOM I was in love with God. . . . Perhaps it was that love that gave me the courage to write it. . . .
>
> Also, I have to believe a few things about what I *thought* was my hatred for God. Its [*sic*] simply the old love/hate relationship. I loved this thing called God so much, hungered for it more than anything in the world, yet felt I was undeserving of Its Love, so I raged at it. Ive [*sic*] also come to believe that the hatred helped keep me alive. It literally energized me. The Latin word from which we get our word, violent, means, Life Force, and I guess that was the only way I could animate that Life Force at that time; i.e, prior to accepting the fact that I Loved this thing called God.[2]

Since it was deliberately written to challenge and provoke middle-class, traditional readers by violating a kind of historical, if unwritten, consensus concerning acceptable taste in fiction, it

UNDERSTANDING HUBERT SELBY, JR.

was hardly surprising that Selby's first novel was greeted in 1964 with considerable controversy. In fact, *Last Exit to Brooklyn* inspired a much-publicized trial for obscenity in England, was debated in the British House of Commons, and was banned in Italy. All of this, of course, contributed to the novel's success; these attempts to censor it undoubtedly resulted in its being noticed and discussed even more than it might otherwise have been. Selby then achieved cult status as a writer, in fact becoming, along with Burroughs, Rechy, and Terry Southern, a leading figure in Grove's stable of underground writers. Seven years later he added to that vision of his work with his second novel, *The Room*. In part inspired by Jean Genet's *Our Lady of the Flowers* (1948, rev. 1951) and if anything even more experimental in form than *Last Exit to Brooklyn, The Room* largely abandons any concept of fictional plot and merges external, or mimetic, "reality" with the psychotic ragings and fantasies of its central, and to a very real extent, only character, an unnamed man jailed for some reason that Selby never makes clear to the reader.

This anonymous prisoner, a characterization which echoes the fiction of Franz Kakfa and Louis-Ferdinand Céline, exemplifies the forgotten and powerless contemporary American urban male. Selby echoes both mainstream American popular culture and its distorted reflection in the subculture of pornography in order to give voice to the truly and deliberately obscene ravings of his protagonist. While inevitably condemned by some critics, *The Room*'s disturbing narrative immediacy gained it the best reviews of any Selby novel, including *Last Exit to Brooklyn,* even though, as its author has himself insisted, its controlling aesthetic of unrelenting blasphemy and rage makes it almost unbearable to read at times: "... *The Room* was the most disturbing book I have ever read. I mean, it is really a disturbing book, Jesus Christ! I didn't read it for twelve years after I wrote it."[3] If *Last Exit to Brooklyn* was intended as an assault upon the citadel of restraint and "good taste" in American fiction, *The Room* constitutes all-out warfare, and it realizes, at times too successfully, in fact, its artistic intentions.

Unfortunately the largely positive reception of *The Room* represents, at least thus far, the high point in Selby's critical and popular acceptance. In 1976 he disappointed many of his early admirers without gaining a significant number of new ones with his third novel, *The Demon*. In distinct contrast to the narrative and stylistic innovations that characterize both *Last Exit to Brooklyn* and *The Room, The Demon* is, in both form and style, a largely conventional novel. Moreover, in it Selby temporarily abandons his familiar lower-class urban setting in favor of a suburban, upper-class world. As a result of these departures from his earlier work, Selby was condemned by some critics for appearing to forget the unique expression of compassion for the economically and spiritually destitute that distinguishes his first two novels and by others for trying and failing to make believable a world about which he knew nothing. In fact, while admittedly the least successful of Selby's five published volumes of fiction, *The Demon* is nevertheless an honest novel containing moments of intense power. It is also crucial to the expression of the aesthetic vision that underlies Selby's work. By focusing upon an affluent but profoundly alienated central character, the novel underscores the essential fact that Selby is not primarily a social protest writer. As diag-

UNDERSTANDING HUBERT SELBY, JR.

nosed in his fiction, the predominantly male disease of alienation and rage has roots more profoundly spiritual than economic.

The Demon describes the fatal madness that results from uncontrollable obsession. Selby's next novel, *Requiem for a Dream,* published two years later in 1978, is devoted to a comparable theme, the destructive nature of addiction. In addition to drug addiction, it is concerned with an even more widespread and more respectable kind of dependency in American life. One of its three central characters is literally driven to insanity by her immersion in American consumerism, as perpetuated by the relentless advertising on television of commercial products. It is probably safe to assume that Selby did not miss the irony when an old ally, Paul Metcalf, accused him of having committed, in writing *Requiem for a Dream,* that most unforgivable sin for an underground writer, having gone "commercial."[4] Metcalf to the contrary notwithstanding, *Requiem* is essential to the completion of Selby's vision.

Three of its four main characters are from the lower rungs of the great American middle class; their initial level of economic security, while certainly fragile, is still real. Thus, until they surrender to their addictions, they have experienced nothing like the brutal, sordid world of *Last Exit to Brooklyn.* The fourth central character comes from and rejects a social position comparable to that held by the protagonist of *The Demon.* Again, Selby's point is that a selfish pride and spiritual emptiness permeates every economic level of American society and is thus beyond the reach of social reform. Moreover, it should be emphasized that *Requiem for a Dream,* however conventional in form it may be, is in fact a very good novel. That it remains as

UNDERSTANDING HUBERT SELBY, JR.

underrated as it does reveals a great deal about the limitations of the present critical response to Selby; having initially defined him as an experimental writer, the critical establishment remains unable to approach his work in any other way.

While Selby has not published a novel in the nineteen years since *Requiem for a Dream,* he produced a collection of short stories, *Song of the Silent Snow,* in 1986 that, while largely unknown, is his most successful work since *Last Exit to Brooklyn.* Both cumulatively and individually, the fifteen stories that make up the volume yield more than one kind of aesthetic reward to the reader. For instance, the collection is subtly but effectively organized: the best of the stories in the first half of the volume often echo, in theme as well as technique, *Last Exit to Brooklyn* and *The Room,* communicating the urban rage and alienation so memorably expressed in these two novels. In contrast, a surprising and for Selby new note of affirmation and hope appears in the last half of the collection. In one recent interview Selby confirms the emergence in these stories of this new hopefulness,[5] while in another he discusses a major shift in his personal vision after *Last Exit to Brooklyn* and *The Room.* He says that he transcended the hatred of God that inspired these first two novels not through any commitment to "organized religion," but rather through faith in a spirituality emanating from "a power of infinite and unconditional love."[6] In this context, he vowed to continue to examine "the disease" of "a lack of love" in America and revealed that he was at work on a novel to be called "Seeds of Pain, Seeds of Love" (301–02). Subsequently, Selby has said that he has temporarily put aside this novel in favor of another that is presently called "The Willow Tree" and will focus on the theme of "redemption through forgiveness."[7]

Overview

Selby's insistence, from the beginning of his career, upon rebelling against the traditional conventions and limitations of mainstream American literature should be examined in the context of the painful and, in fact, nearly fatal experiences of his adolescence and early manhood. He can perhaps best be understood in the context of the group of American novelists—including Jack London, James Jones, Nelson Algren, and Rechy among others—who can be described as "social outlaws."Selby was born in Victory Memorial Hospital in Brooklyn on July 23, 1928. He has said that his parents, Hubert, Sr., an engineer, and Adalin (Layne) Selby, then lived "near 8th Avenue" and were middle class "in the same way that ninety-five percent of Americans during the Depression were middle-class." He graduated from P.S. 102 and attended Peter Stuyvesant High School for one year before dropping out in 1944 at the age of fifteen and to serve as an oiler with the Merchant Marine.[8] While stationed in Europe, he became ill with tuberculosis in 1947 and for the next three and a half years spend most of his time in various hospitals and other institutions in New York.[9] Before he was medically released to return to the States in 1950, he "had ten ribs cut out, lung problems, and asthma" (Vorda 289). Responding in a 1992 interview to a question of whether the obsession with death that runs throughout his fiction began then to preoccupy him, Selby said:

You spend 3+ years in bed and it affects your life and everything that affects your life affects your work. I also believe that you don't understand life until you die or come close to dying. That may have a lot to do with the nature of my writing. Lying in bed also gives you a greater opportunity than usual to look inside yourself and find out exactly what's going on. I had never read a book until then. That's where it all started: reading and then a desire to write. (Vorda 289)

It was also during this period that Selby's experience with narcotics began, a matter he frankly addresses in the 1992 interview: "When I was in the hospital, I had a lot of drugs such as morphine, demerol, codeine, and various sleeping pills. I also used heroin. I also drank every opportunity I could . . ." (Vorda 292). Not surprisingly, all this dependence led to his addiction, which in turn led at one point to his arrest: "The reason I was in jail was for possession of narcotics. Heroin. [The actual charge was driving while under the influence.] The drugs were an extension of all the addictive medication I had when I was in the hospital" (Vorda 297).[10]

Back in New York in 1950 and determined to write though lacking even a high-school education, Selby met and soon became one of a group of young rebel writers, several of whom had attended Black Mountain College. Gilbert Sorrentino, who would be one of Selby's closest friends, was central to the group, which also counted Amiri Baraka (then LeRoi Jones), Joel Oppenheimer, Robert Creely, and Joe Early among its members. In 1988 Selby, who was nicknamed Cubby as a boy, recalled these years of his literary apprenticeship with pleasurable nostalgia: "Oh, it was great! I knew a lot of painters and musicians. We used to spend every weekend at LeRoi's house: and there might be anybody from Edward Dahlberg to Cecil Taylor [there]" (Langenheim 19). The informal group, which already thought of itself as constituting an artistic counterculture, formed several little magazines—for example, *Yugen, NEON,* and *THE FLOATING BEAR.* In a recent letter Selby affirms his friendship with and admiration of Sorrentino: "He is not only a life long friend, but my literary mentor."[11]

Involvement with small "underground" literary magazines quickly became crucial for Selby, who, encouraged and helped by Sorrentino and Jones, began publishing in such journals as *Black Mountain Review, New Directions,* and *Provincetown Review.* He also sold a story to the commercial men's magazine *Swank.* These publications, as obscure as they might have been to mainstream American readers, gained Selby an audience and caught the attention of Grove Press; and ultimately, in revised form, they would become the core of *Last Exit to Brooklyn.* "Tralala" appeared in *Provincetown Review,* where it came to the attention of Barney Rosset at Grove.[12] Rosset then helped its author produce *Last Exit to Brooklyn* and quickly moved to take advantage of some controversy surrounding the novel's reception. In 1990 Selby fondly recalled his publisher's instincts for promoting *Last Exit to Brooklyn.* He remembered that while the novel received largely positive reviews, *Time*'s review attacked it as "'Grove's dirty book of the month,'" which encouraged *Newsweek* not only to praise but even to help publicize it:

And then Barney took out this big full-page ad in the [New York] *Times,* and I remember . . . in big caps, they had a quote from Allen Ginsberg and it was something like: "THIS BOOK SHOULD EXPLODE LIKE A RUSTY BOMBSHELL OVER AMERICA." And that certainly didn't do any harm. Then it had a whole bunch of quotes from people. And they really pushed it. . . . I understand they sold out the first edition before publication date. (Gontarski 113)

In fact, as Selby remembered in 1990, "Tralala" occasioned controversy immediately upon its appearance in *Provincetown Review:*

. . . in Provincetown the local court arrested the editor . . . for selling pornographic literature to a minor, and it turned out the minor wasn't a minor; he was nineteen years old. Turns out it was all a kind of setup. And the thing was so flagrantly illegal that after he was found guilty in a lower court, the state attorney threw it out, and then the *Provincetown Review* printed the transcript of the whole trial. (Gontarski 114)

Then *Last Exit to Brooklyn*'s history of controversy and censorship culminated in the novel's being banned in Italy. It was hardly surprising, given his personal experiences—growing up in Brooklyn, in Europe as a member of the Merchant Marine, and later with the Sorrentino-Jones group of literary rebels—that Selby would emerge as a writer speaking for an American

UNDERSTANDING HUBERT SELBY, JR.

counterculture that began with the Beat Generation in the 1950s and exploded in the 1960s. The attacks upon and attempted censorship of his first novel merely intensified his already-formulated aesthetic perspective.

In *Last Exit to Brooklyn* he treated subject matter that had been ignored or, perhaps worse, distorted and sometimes even glamorized in the accepted canon of American literature—homosexuality, transvestitism, and roving urban street gangs—with unrelenting and often brutal realism. He continued his exploration of taboo subjects and of ignored, if not actually repressed, subcultures within American society in his next four volumes of fiction. Still it is not his subject matter that defines Selby as a profoundly revolutionary American writer; rather it is his intuitive understanding of the nature of power in American society and his determination to give voice to the powerless. Moreover, the voice he has given his outcasts is harsh, cruel, and often deeply profane; and he presents it with little narrative mediation to soften it or make it more conventionally acceptable. In this way Selby has concluded the naturalist literary agenda that began with Stephen Crane and Frank Norris in the last years of the nineteenth century, while simultaneously perfecting his own highly innovative brand of fiction.

CHAPTER TWO

Last Exit to Brooklyn

In part because of the British censorship of the novel and such hostile American reviews as *Time*'s, *Last Exit to Brooklyn* quickly gained a reputation as an "underground classic." Yet it remains largely neglected in critical studies of the contemporary American novel. Two important exceptions to this neglect are Josephine Hendin's *Vulnerable People: A View of American Fiction since 1945* (1978) and Gerd Hurm's *Fragmented Urban Images: The American City in Modern Fiction from Stephen Crane to Thomas Pynchon* (1991). In addition, Tony Tanner briefly discusses *Last Exit to Brooklyn* in his seminal 1971 study of the post–World War II American novel, *City of Words: American Fiction 1950–1970*. Hendin's feminist study emphasizes the male sadism and violence that runs throughout Selby's work: "The relentless pursuit of machismo through all the ways of cruelty, the fear of failure and worthlessness that drives men into deeper and deeper vileness are Selby's preoccupations. He is a clinician of male violence, dissecting straight to the center of sexual chaos and cruelty."[1] This analysis's emphasis on the degree to which violence in Selby's work expresses the damaged and perverted sexuality of his male characters is especially perceptive.

Hurm's chapter on *Last Exit to Brooklyn* in *Fragmented Urban Images* is one of the most extensive, and important, treatments of the novel to appear thus far. By comparing Selby's novel to Stephen Crane's *Maggie: A Girl of the Streets,* Hurm perceptively analyzes *Last Exit to Brooklyn* as being naturalistic in theme but highly modernistic in technique. In fact, he argues that one can detect a comparable surrealistic quality in the fiction of Crane and Selby. Neither writer is fundamentally devoted to the documentation and detail that Emile Zola prescribed as being goals of the naturalistic writer, but each does subscribe to the traditional philosophic center of literary naturalism, a belief in determinism. Inevitably, given the quite different times in which they lived, their views of determinism are hardly identical. As Crane made clear in his inscriptions of gift copies of *Maggie* to Hamlin Garland and others, he at least intended his novel to convey to middle-class readers the revolutionary idea that "street girls" are victims of the slum and thus deserving of moral, even Christian, forgiveness.[2] Determinism is just as central to Selby's work, which depicts characters so obsessed by hatred and self-loathing that any external forgiveness is meaningless to them; the people of *Last Exit to Brooklyn* are victimized by the cruel environment in which they are trapped and also by the existential absurdity of the universe itself.[3]

In addition to this crucial difference in moral perspective, there is, as Hurm describes, another basic reason that Selby inevitably produced a different kind of work than Crane had. The New York City slum had undergone profound changes since the turn of the century:

> the record of urban experience in Brooklyn is a reaction to Crane's portrayal of the Lower East Side in the 1890s. *Last Exit to Brooklyn* deals with the transition from the old street-corner slum of squalid tenements to the ameliorated

surroundings of the low-income housing projects of the 1950s which liberal sociologists and planners had suggested to improve the lot of the urban underprivileged. Though projecting environmental changes, Selby shows that, even in new buildings, the dwellers remain trapped.[4]

In fact, as Hurm discusses, the improved chances for sheer economic survival that Selby's people enjoy only intensify their rage. America in the 1950s was generally prosperous and, after the rationing and other sacrifices during World War II, committed to the materialistic values of an emerging consumerism. The inhabitants of Selby's slum, while certainly aware of and attracted to the new consumerism, are denied an equal opportunity to participate in it. Their anger at those who enjoy that privilege is then understandable.

Still, it is important to stress that Selby's characters are irrevocably trapped by internal as well as by external factors. Indeed, they suffer from an irreversible death of the soul. It is worth mentioning that two extremely astute observers of contemporary American fiction missed this vital spiritual dimension of *Last Exit*. Tony Tanner, in *City of Words,* simplistically dismisses Selby's novel. While praising the novel for the "anti-elegant harsh-edged directness" of its "style,"[5] he attempts to explain Selby's complex novel from a limited sociological-anthropological perspective as a human example of a "behavioral sink":

A good way to describe what Selby is doing is to say that he is trying to depict a human version of what the ecologist John Calhoun called a "behavioral sink." In a "behavioral sink" all normal patterns of behavior are disrupted, and the unusual stress leads to all forms of perversion, violence, and breakdown. This is what happens when too many animals are crowded into too little territory. (345)

Tanner concludes his analysis by remarking that *Last Exit to Brooklyn* "makes realism too crude" (348).

Three years later Joyce Carol Oates issued a comparable criticism of Selby's novel. In an essay on Harriette Arnow's *The Dollmaker,* she congratulates Arnow for insisting upon a spiritual dimension underlying the economic suffering and degradation in her novel, which takes place in the inner-city Detroit of the Great Depression. In contrast, Oates dismisses "the frantic naturalism" of Selby's novel, which "would give us, probably, a more truthful vision of Detroit, then and now; but such naturalism, totally absorbed in an analysis of bodily existence is . . . unfaithful to the spiritual and imaginative demands that some people, at least, still make."[6] It is difficult to know exactly what Oates means here, especially if one remembers that setting and incident are so deliberately exaggerated in Selby's book that they can hardly be equated with a recognizable empirical "reality." As Hurm points out, the prose in *Last Exit to Brooklyn* is a "poetic," surrealistic transformation of reality rather than a literal recording of it.

Selby has directly responded to Tanner's analysis. In a 1992 interview he denies that he was trying, in his first novel, to create "a human behavioral sink" and insists that his fiction should not be viewed as a sociological or anthropological experiment, but instead as a mode of putting his readers through an "emotional experience" by involving them in the pain and suffering of "real people."[7] Oates's criticism can be read as implying that the inhabitants of Selby's world are unaware of anything beyond mere "bodily existence."

In one of the earliest critical discussions of *Last Exit to Brooklyn,* Charles D. Peavy also denies, though for quite different reasons than Oates's, that Selby's characters enjoy genuine humanity. Peavy describes Selby as being a kind of Swiftian satirist who deliberately creates "subhuman," if "recognizable," creatures in order to emphasize the deadly nature of "the sin of pride."[8]

Indeed, awareness of "the sin of pride" is crucial to a full understanding of *Last Exit,* as is Peavy's perception that Selby's creations are more disturbing than Swift's because they consistently exhibit distorted and even savage behavior. Still, it should not be forgotten that Selby's aesthetic insists upon the essential humanness of his characters.

One reason for *Last Exit to Brooklyn*'s disturbing effect when it first appeared in 1964 was that it brought to an abrupt and shocking conclusion the program instituted by American literary naturalism in the late nineteenth century. Inspired primarily by Emile Zola, Frank Norris in *McTeague* (1899) and the posthumously published *Vandover and the Brute* (1914) launched an attack on the tradition of the American novel as a refined and genteel artifact. A central element in Norris's agenda, at least during the first part of his career, was to challenge a long-standing tradition in American literature that, while human behavior might in fact descend on occasion to shocking and even disgusting depths, the American writer should ignore such aberrations. Norris was quickly followed by Jack London, who suggested in *The People of the Abyss* (1903) that the extreme poverty of London's East End had transformed that city's underclass into a new and subhuman "race" and then argued in his next book, *The Call of the Wild* (1903), that civilized morality was a fragile and artificial construct. Even before Norris and London, Stephen Crane had, in *Maggie: A Girl of the Streets* (1893, 1896), created a fictional world in which the "characters" are depicted as intellectually primitive puppets of the environment in which they are trapped.

Throughout the modernist period such American novelists as William Faulkner, Ernest Hemingway, John Dos Passos, and Nelson Algren were fascinated by grotesque and brutal manifestations of human behavior. Still, prior to *Last Exit to Brooklyn,* no American novelist had given a largely unmediated voice to psychotic characters driven by all-consuming rage and hatred. Selby's truly unique contribution to the American novel was to conclude the turn-of-the-century American naturalists' assault on a dominant literature of artificial gentility by wedding their goal with a distinctly European aesthetic as practiced by such existentialists as Franz Kafka, Louis-Ferdinand Céline, and Jean Genet.[9] The fiction that results from this aesthetic documents the inherent absurdity of characters while still insisting upon their essential humanity. Perhaps the most shocking aspect of Selby's fiction is its implication that humanness does not, in itself, guarantee redemption and transcendence.

Peavy and Oates to the contrary, the characters of *Last Exit to Brooklyn* are "real people"; they are simply unlike any people that had previously appeared in the American novel. This difference originates in the aesthetic of rage and hate that underlies their creation. It seems clear that this aesthetic grew out of the brutal and nearly fatal events of Selby's early years. In his revealing 1981 interview with John O'Brien, Selby says that when he was eighteen, he "was very bitter and very angry." That he experienced such self-destructive bitterness, he explains, allows him to understand and write about the anonymous and paranoid protagonist of his second novel, *The Room,* and the predatory prostitute, Tralala, who appears in *Last Exit to Brooklyn.* [10] Selby's complex love-hate relationship with God seems to control the narrative perspective of both *Last Exit to Brooklyn* and *The Room.*

It is important to distinguish Selby's "hatred" from the kind of predominantly rational rejection of God that is central to so much modern Western literature and philosophy. Certainly the novelist would discover in Nietzsche, Sartre and others an intellectual foundation for his position; but his rage was already present. Hatred of God was not for the early Selby a deliberately chosen intellectual stance, but a deeply personal response to the brutality of the world and to his own personal lapses and transgressions. Such a response might easily have resulted in artistic chaos and disaster if Selby had not recognized, despite his personal hatred and pain, the necessity of a spiritual dimension in human life, and the redeeming potential of love. This recognition, in turn, enabled him to impose a deceptive, but nevertheless more than sufficient, control on his material. As a result Selby's fiction is a much more complex achievement than it has been recognized to be largely because it subtly reconciles conflicting emotions and feelings.

LAST EXIT TO BROOKLYN

An experimental and episodic work made up of segments related primarily by thematic vision and setting, *Last Exit to Brooklyn* focuses on three independent characters and two cumulative characterizations that illustrate in different ways the deadening, and in fact sometimes literally deadly, consequences of living in a world that denies God and rejects love. First there is the "hip" drag queen Georgette who, more openly and unapologetically than any other character in the novel, seeks love. Though she has at least as much reason as any other character in the novel to feel it, Georgette is something of an aberrational character simply because she rejects a consuming hatred in order to pursue her quest for love. She thus emerges as the book's most overtly sympathetic character. Selby has said that his compassion for Georgette comes through so clearly in *Last Exit to Brooklyn* that it had the unexpected result of making many readers assume that he was himself gay.[11]

While heterosexual, Selby—along with another Grove Press author, John Rechy, whose revolutionary gay novel *City of Night* appeared the year before *Last Exit to Brooklyn*—broke new ground in American fiction by treating the drag queen as a sympathetic character. In his 1992 interview with Alan Vorda, the novelist discusses his sympathetic treatment of Georgette, as well as the character's centrality to his novel:

> There was a real kid named George. Georgie must have felt like an outcast who was totally alienated. He was hysterical in his defense; and his defense was hysteria. And the more he fed that with stimulants, the more hysterical and wacky and flighty he became. I've always felt like an outcast who

was alienated all my life. So Georgie and I had that point of identification although this was totally unconscious. I had a tremendous sympathy for George. I felt like my life was fucking ruined and a disaster. So I had this empathy, sympathy, and compassion going for Georgie.

. . . A year or two later I met someone from the old neighborhood and they said Georgie had been found dead in the street, evidently an O.D. He was only about twenty years old when he died. . . . I guess I felt Georgie needed more than a death in the street. He needed a memorial. . . . Thus, in a very real way, Georgie is responsible for the book *Last Exit to Brooklyn.* (293)

The narrative voice in the novel makes it clear that Georgette is to be admired as much for the sheer honesty of her lifestyle as for her valiant quest for love:

She (he) didnt try to disguise or conceal [her homosexuality] . . . with marriage and mans talk, satisfying her homosexuality with the keeping of a secret scrapbook of pictures of favorite male actors or athletes or by supervising the activities of young boys or visiting turkish baths or mens locker rooms, leering sidely while seeking protection behind a carefully guarded guise of virility. . . .[12]

Georgette, like many drag queens, is in love with the idea of costume, seeing in it the possibility of adopting a new, and always slightly shifting, identity. Thus she seeks salvation in an ongoing process of constant external change that originates, ironically, in a willed stability. She has bravely chosen to create from within an identity that denies those aspects of external reality that are unbearable to her.

Nevertheless her valiant quest for love and salvation is doomed by the final impossibility of transcending her environment and by her own acceptance of certain of its values. Tragically she chooses a sadistic young punk named Vinnie as the embodiment of her dream of a saving love. It can be argued that one of the qualities that makes Georgette admirable is also the central factor in her destruction—just as she chooses not to let her gender dictate her willed identity, she chooses to ignore the undeniable and considerable evidence of Vinnie's selfishness and brutality. He responds to her offers of affection by mentally and physically assaulting her.

The Georgette-Vinnie relationship is one of the clearest illustrations in the novel of Selby's debt to Stephen Crane. Crane's Maggie of *Maggie: A Girl of the Streets,* like Georgette, is blind to the cruel shallowness of her chosen "knight," Pete the bartender, until it is too late. There is, though, one significant difference in the failure of Crane's and Selby's characters to perceive the true nature of the young men whom they adore. Maggie's idealization of Pete seems to originate primarily in her simple ignorance and inexperience. In contrast Georgette's determination to perceive Vinnie as an ideal lover is essential to her attempted construction of an alternate, and bearable, reality. Since from the very first he publicly ridicules and derides her, she cannot be unaware, on some level, of his viciousness.

Again like Crane's heroine, Georgette brings about her own destruction, to a degree, through her fascination with American popular culture, especially Hollywood films. She views Vinnie as a romantic young outlaw in the mode of John Garfield and other 1940s movie stars. Most of Selby's characters, in fact, are thoroughly indoctrinated with the values implicit in Hollywood films and American pulp fiction. Moreover Vinnie has himself created a superficial persona based upon the same sources. At the age of fifteen he was "arrested for the 11th time . . . [and] sent to a correctional institution for boys" (26). The next year he was "sent up for his first real bit" after stealing a car and wrecking it on Ocean Parkway while attempting to see how fast it could go (26). This punishment hardly serves to reform him: "He seemed to enjoy the time he spent in jail. While there he tattooed his number on his wrist with a pin and ink and displayed it to everyone when he came home" (27). Shortly after his release he reads in the paper that a man he knew in prison has been killed while attempting an armed robbery: "The glory of having known someone killed by the police during a stickup was the greatest event of his life and a memory he cherished as would an aging invalid, at the end of a disappointing life, a winning touchdown at the end of the final game of the season" (27–28).

As Selby people, Georgette and Vinnie seek escape from their powerlessness and boredom in imagined alternate realities; such escapes, needless to say, will always fail for a character who, like Georgette, possesses any genuine intelligence and sensitivity. They, in fact, only work for dull, cruel, and unimaginative hoodlums such as Vinnie. The climax of Vinnie's humiliation and destruction of Georgette occurs at a sordid party given by

Georgette and three of her drag queen friends for Vinnie, Harry, and Malfie, three members of the vicious street gang that constitutes a cumulative character and serves to unify the novel. Georgette convinces herself that this will be the romantic evening during which Vinnie will finally announce and demonstrate his love for her.

A key passage from one of the not-infrequent moments in which Georgette deliberately slips into an artificially "romantic" discourse indicates the degree to which she is determined to ignore any unpleasant aspects of reality and to view Vinnie's abundant weaknesses as strengths:

> I mean the candlelight and everything . . . it brings to mind Genet. . . .
>
> [Vinnie interrupts:] Whose this junay?
>
> [Georgette answers:] A french writer Vinnie. I am certain you would not know about such things. . . . She creates such beauty out of the tortured darkness of our souls . . . and I feel so beautiful. (53–54)

She incorporates the young hoodlum's crudeness and ignorance into her image of him as a tough, but loving, young criminal—after all, the characters that Garfield and James Cagney usually played in films were generally not readers or thinkers.

During the party Vinnie does momentarily feel something for Georgette. While the music of Charlie Parker is being heard in the background and everyone is high on drugs, the hopelessly romantic drag queen recites Poe's "The Raven." The very strangeness of this entire experience penetrates Vinnie's shield of toughness, and he is mystified by the quite foreign tenderness and concern for Georgette that he feels. As quickly as he possibly can, he retreats from the vulnerability to which such positive and genuine feelings reduce him and finds refuge in the presence of the other gang members:

> Vinnie struggled with the softness he felt, . . . battling with his boundaries then saying, Hey, that was alright Georgie boy, then the knowledge of his friends being there, especially Harry, forced its way through the bennie and the mood and he sat back quickly, took a drink and grubbed a smoke from Harry. (66–67)

Inevitably Vinnie loses the battle with "his boundaries" and, before the party ends, emotionally assaults and humiliates Georgette again. Like most of Selby's characters, he has erected a barrier around his persona that generally succeeds in denying any and all forms of "softness." It is significant that, at the moment when his hardness begins to crack, he turns to members of the gang, and especially to Harry, for vindication and support. As Selby's work progressed, "Harry" became the most common name for his embittered and powerless urban Everyman; for instance, his 1986 short-story collection, *Song of the Silent Snow,* evokes eight Harrys (plus two Harolds) representing virtually all levels of society. The young gang member from whom Harry begs a smoke is a recurring figure in *Last Exit to Brooklyn* and is, moreover, the first of two or possibly three Harrys in the novel.

Georgette's segment of the novel ends with the drag queen's attempting to deny Vinnie's latest violation of her trust and affection: "Yes my love, I hear him. Yes. He is blowing love" (81). The reader knows that, despite her determination to deny reality, her courageous and determined quest for love will end and that its end will mean her destruction. It is worth noting that in Uli Edel's excellent 1989 film version of *Last Exit,* for which Selby served as an adviser, Georgette *is* killed when she rushes out into a street and is run over by a cab. Selby played the cabdriver. It is also implicit in the novel that the drag queen is doomed, as would be any inhabitant of Selby's world so determined to cling to an illusion of romance.

In a quite different way Tralala, a simultaneously victimized and frightening and rapacious character, is also trapped by an illusion of romance. Clearly the characterization of Tralala represented a radical and shocking departure from traditional American literature. To understand how much so, one need only recall three of her fictional predecessors. It is true that Crane's Maggie is not especially intelligent, but she is still a sympathetic, even an idealized, figure who turns to prostitution only after an innocent, but doomed, pursuit of American middle-class values.[13] In *The Sun Also Rises* Ernest Hemingway goes to some trouble to explain the origins of the seeming callousness of Lady Brett Ashley, and, of course, this prototype of hedonism famously decides, in the concluding section of the novel, not to be "a bitch." John Steinbeck's Cathy Trask of *East of Eden* (1952) anticipates Tralala in her absence of emotion and her capacity for cruelty. In several places in the novel Steinbeck's narrator explains Cathy as a monstrous freak of nature, a kind of twentieth-century manifestation of the witches who haunted medieval Europe as well as the Puritans of the Massachusetts Bay colony.

In contrast there is nothing idealistic, redemptive, or supernatural in Selby's depiction of Tralala. She appears to have accepted the commodification of her body almost instinctively, deciding early that exploiting society's dehumanization was an easy way not only to survive, but to ward off the boredom inevitably attendant upon a total submersion in materiality:

> Tralala was 15 the first time she was laid. There was no real passion. Just diversion. . . . she got what she wanted. All she had to do was putout. It was kicks too. Sometimes. If not, so what? It made no difference. Lay on your back. Or bend over a garbage can. Better than working. And its kicks. For a while anyway. But time always passes. (97)

Perhaps the most truly upsetting aspect of this account of Tralala's teenage sexual exploitation is her passive cooperation in it. It is as if she has, virtually from the beginning, accepted society's evaluation of her as garbage; she seems never to have had sufficient will to assert her essential humanity. There is a kind of ethical laziness at the core of her characterization; one feels that acting in an affirmative and self-preserving manner would simply require too much effort from her. This does not negate, however, her victimization by an exploitative environment.

She sometimes acts with senseless savagery and cruelty. She has, for instance, established a partnership with two of the street gang members, Al and Tony, in which she tempts victims into abandoned alleys and lots where they are brutally subdued and beaten by Al and Tony before being robbed. The three especially like to prey on lonely soldiers from the Brooklyn army base. In one particularly savage instance she herself initiates the physical brutality, knocking a young soldier unconscious with a bottle and then stealing his wallet. Later, when the desperate young man comes into the Greeks (the all-night diner where she and the gang spend their time between criminal acts) to beg not for the return of his wallet or his money, but only for the identification he must have in order to return to the base, Tony and Al beat him until he is barely conscious. Then Tralala completes the savage assault: "Before they left Tralala stomped on his face until both eyes were bleeding and his nose was split and broken then kicked him a few times in the balls" (99).

It is difficult to think of a female character in American literature before Tralala who could or would engage in such cold, emotionless savagery. She has so accepted the dominant society's view of her as mere body that she has contributed significantly to the death of her soul. Acts of senseless cruelty and violence have become her way of coping with society's denial of her self and with the sheer banality of an existence devoted entirely to the physical, an existence devoid of any redemptive spirituality. Ironically the central complexity in Selby's characterization of Tralala begins when she is unexpectedly confronted with the possibility of precisely this kind of redemption. She meets and spends three days and nights with an army officer who buys her expensive presents and shows her Manhattan, a world as foreign and exotic to Tralala as a remote tropical island, and then abruptly tells her that he is leaving to go overseas. Before his departure the officer gives her an envelope containing not money as the prostitute hopes and expects, but a letter expressing his love for her.

After reading only part of the letter, Tralala is enraged and confused. She has anticipated valorization of her body in the only way she knows and can easily comprehend: in an act of materialistic tribute. Thus she is angry at being cheated out of the money she feels she has earned and more than a little frightened by the officer's promise of love. He has briefly shown her a system of values that can only reflect a world of sensitivity and caring that she has not previously encountered. She can understand, and even feel vaguely grateful for, one particular bit of praise that the officer gives her before leaving. He expresses, in the language of crude masculinity, admiration for her breasts: "he turned and kissed her and told her she had the most beautiful pair of tits he had ever seen" (102). One remembers Pete's comparable expression of admiration for Maggie in Crane's novel: "'Say, Mag, I'm stuck on yer shape. It's outa sight. . . .'"[14] Crane and Selby appear to be making essentially the same point: women who have been so dehumanized as to accept the commodification of their bodies invite and even encourage the most primitive expressions of admiration.

While Tralala reacts in a different way to her defining experience with the army officer than Maggie does to her encounter with Pete, she just as irrevocably moves toward her final, literal destruction. In an act of rage and fury she tears up the officer's letter and proceeds to seek tributes to her body in progressively more dingy and sordid bars, from Manhattan back to her home territory of Brooklyn. At one point she is forcefully ejected from a bar in Manhattan and warned against ever attempting to return. This incident highlights the dominant and sustaining vision of Selby's novel; hostile and claustrophobic in nature, the world of Brooklyn irrevocably holds and perverts the people whom it produces. In sharp contrast to Crane's brief and detached account of Maggie's descent into prostitution and inevitable destruction, Selby narrates Tralala's disintegration in grim and sordid detail:

Time passed—months, maybe years, who knows, and the dress was gone and just a beatup skirt and sweater and the Broadway bars were 8th avenue bars, but soon even these joints with their hustlers, pushers, pimps, queens and wouldbe thugs kicked her out and the inlaid linoleum turned to wood and then was covered with sawdust and she hung over a beer in a dump on the waterfront, snarling and cursing every sonofabitch who fucked herup and left with anyone who looked at her or had a place to flop. (108)

Unlike Crane, Selby intends no idealization in the characterization of his prostitute; he goes to some narrative lengths to make certain that virtually nothing even remotely affirmative can be detected in her brief, ugly existence. As the novel's objective narration makes inevitable, the motivation behind her self-destruction after the affair with the army officer is left somewhat vague. A probable interpretation is that the officer, by revealing to her a world so foreign to anything she has ever known before, a world in which women can be genuinely loved rather than merely commodified, has unwittingly challenged the only value system Tralala has ever known. For two related reasons the concept of such a redemptive world proves literally destructive for her.

First, an undeniable implication of the officer's letter is that in the world outside Brooklyn the cold, materialistic manner in which Tralala has always related to men is not the only possible mode of interaction between the sexes. Yet it is the only kind she has observed in the predatory inner city of her experience. Thus the officer's suggestion of a relationship based on love inevitably carries with it the implication that her past has been a futile and sordid story of cynical surrender to environmental exploitation. For Tralala the possibility that her life might have been different and even worthwhile had she lived in a different time and place and possessed more strength and at least some degree of spiritual pride is too much to bear. Unwilling to undertake the required struggle, she retreats from the challenge of spiritual redemption and instead wraps herself in the kind of selfish pride that is central to the destruction of most Selby characters. In a perceptive essay about the 1989 film version of *Last Exit to Brooklyn,* Richard Gehr describes the novel's various segments as "blunt, naturalistic moral fables."[15] It is true that, while all the characters in the novel are victimized by a brutal environment, they are guilty of moral failures that make their victimization complete and irrevocable.

Second, it is at least possible that the officer has touched some residue of real and affirmative feeling in Tralala that has become so foreign to her conscious self that she does not know how to respond to it. Again, the deliberately restricted manner of the novel's narration makes it impossible to be really certain about any of Tralala's motivations; the reader can only try to comprehend her characterization on the basis of her spoken

words and actions and the most superficial level of her consciousness. But it may be surmised that, if the officer has indeed touched
some vestigial sense of romance in Tralala, she, in a rage rooted
in the deepest frustration, knows only to demand repeated affirmation of the beauty of her breasts, the one expression of
affection and praise from the officer that she truly understands.

Finally, in drunken desperation, she returns to familiar
territory, a cheap bar she has worked in the past: "She could
get a seamans whole payoff just sittin in Willies. People knew
who she was in Willies" (109). But her extended period of
senseless dissipation has taken such a toll on her appearance
that even in Willies she is considered damaged goods. In fact,
no one particularly notices her until she bares her breasts and
taunts the men in the bar with them. It is worth noting that the
novel, in describing this act of desperate exhibitionism,
affirms that Tralala exposes "her pride to the bar" (113). Now
mindlessly, yet arrogantly, committed to the material, she seems
deliberately to provoke her final hideous fate—a nightmarish
destruction through sexual intercourse with a seemingly endless
gang of men in the back seat of an abandoned car.

The account of this savagery is almost unbearable in its
detail. Tralala, who was allowed, however briefly and inar-
ticulately, a glimpse of existence beyond the physical, dies as
a result of prolonged assault by brutal materiality; her body
is left alone in a filthy lot, desecrated by increasingly grotesque acts of violent abuse and covered with semen, urine,
and blood. Thus she dies as she has lived, a wasted and
embittered receptacle of the material and the savage. The
generally excellent and faithful 1989 film adaptation of *Last*

Exit to Brooklyn allowed Tralala, brilliantly played by Jennifer Jason Leigh, to survive and even triumph over this final assault. Apparently Uli Eden decided that audiences (and probably censors) would not accept the extreme and grotesque brutality of the scene as Selby had originally written it. Richard Gehr correctly describes Tralala's survival as the film adaptation's "sole false note" (48). Certainly, in both the novel and the film, her total characterization is a deliberate challenge to readers whose taste has been formed by traditional British and American literature.

A comparable challenge is implicit in the character of Harry Black, who is surely one of the most self-centered and least heroic figures to be found in any novel. It is, in fact, the totality of Harry's powerlessness that despite the character's selfishness and weakness demands sympathy from the reader. Both internally and externally he is relentlessly provoked by challenges to his essential human worth and dignity. The product of a working class society in which homophobia runs deep, he finds himself suddenly tortured by homosexual needs and desires. He has grown up, like most of the novel's male characters, hating "queers;" and such unwanted urges can only push him in the direction of self-hatred. Indeed hatred and barely subdued rage have long been the strongest elements in Harry's sexuality. Married and the father of an infant, he is infuriated by his wife's body and her sexual demands, only able to endure intercourse with her by conceiving of it as a form of assault. This defense mechanism produces ironic results: he is "unaware that his brutality in bed was the one thing that kept his wife clinging to him" (120). It is worth repeating here that Selby has been critically chided for objectifying and narratively assaulting female characters, especially in his first three novels. It becomes difficult at times to draw a clear line between Selby's thematic focus upon society's exploitation of women and his seeming approbation of that exploitation.

At any rate the name of Harry's wife is symbolically significant—she is the first of several "Marys" in Selby's fiction. The name "Mary" in his work serves a function comparable to "Harry"; it becomes a code for the universal female, or rather the hostile male perception of such a mythic creature. Despite its obvious and intended Christian overtones, "Mary" functions for Selby as an ironic signifier for a countermyth, the female as trap for the male. In fact, few writers communicate as directly and harshly as Selby a male vision of the woman as a hated and feared "Other," the very image of a corrupt and corrupting trap for the male. In Selby such hatred and fear focuses on the female genitalia; for his male characters who loudly and profanely proclaim the cult of machismo, the vagina both tempts as instrument of pleasure and threatens as origin of defilement and disease. Though they, of course, would never say or admit it, female genitalia portend castration and death. In language as well as action it must be repeatedly assaulted and punished. Thus the woman, rather than representing the divinity of motherhood and new life, literally embodies the threat of impotence and death. In a world without redemptive spiritually and encased in an overwhelming materiality, the concept of a holy mother and virgin, or of a redemptive sexuality, is foreign and incomprehensible.

Harry Black's fate is sealed from the first because, unlike the psychotic street gang members who ultimately assault and destroy him, he cannot avoid confronting the clear implications of his hatred of the female body. Moreover he not only knows about but verbally participates in the homophobia that is not just an accepted but a required expression of the society that produced him. The reader can probably assume that on at least some level his marriage was a desperate attempt to control his "unnatural" and socially unforgivable responses. For a time he succeeded in suppressing them, but after a horrifying dream they become immediate and threatening. In the dream Harry is attacked by the Harpies, dark, sinister figures with "gigantic wings" and "large sharp beaks": "The Harpies swooped down on Harry and in the darkness under their wings he could see nothing but their eyes: small, and filled with hatred, their eyes laughing at him, mocking him as he tried to evade them, knowing he couldnt and that they could toy with him before they slowly destroyed him" (124).

At least in part the Harpies represent Harry's terror at, and loathing for, the still-unarticulated feelings and urges that are torturing him. Already he senses that in some unimaginably horrific way they will consume him: "the Harpies still mocked him as they tore the flesh from his belly, his chest, and scraped their beaks on his ribs and suddenly thrust their beaks into his eyes and plucked them from their sockets" (124). For someone of Harry's lower-class background, the implications of his still-suppressed desires are so terrifying that they cannot be "seen" or realized; in fact, it would be better to have one's eyes plucked out than to acknowledge them. His idea of the world and morality, like that of the surrounding society, rests upon a hypocritical assertion of binary oppositions; it pretends to be, and even believes itself to be, an ethically "white" and "black" world in which there is nothing darker or more unforgivable than homosexuality.

Harry's desperation is intensified by the fact that marriage and sexuality do not constitute the only trap in which he seems hopelessly caught. There is also the inherently boring and meaningless factory job at which he is aggressively incompetent: "He was the worst lathe operator of the more than 1,000 men working in the factory" (126). Believing that his union position as shop steward protects him from retaliation, he has transformed his incompetence into a kind of aggression; he gets some enjoyment in doing his work badly, while knowing that his bosses cannot retaliate against him. Selby's work often echoes ideas formulated by the French philosopher Michel Foucault. For instance, the underlying vision in his novels and stories is concerned in the most fundamental way with power and power structures. In *Last Exit to Brooklyn* sex, work, and the life of the streets all revolve around structures of power; and in all these cases the victimized have surrendered their souls to oppressive social structures and to the rage and hatred that necessarily result from the realization of one's essential powerlessness and insignificance. The real sin of Harry Black and most of Selby's characters is that they lack the strength and conviction to resist such profoundly self-defeating emotions.

Prior to his final destruction, Harry is granted a brief reprieve in both his personal and his professional life. He even transcends his terror of the avenging "Harpies" and his own hatred of "queers" sufficiently to become sexually involved with drag queens whose love of excess and costume excites him. Moreover, when a prolonged work stoppage is called at the factory, he is permitted the illusion of responsibility when he is asked to run strike headquarters (the truth is that no one else wants to be bothered with the job). Harry glories in assigning the petty duties associated with the work at the headquarters. While it is by now impossible for him to escape the hostile persona that he has labored so hard to create, he actually believes that the strike leaders are fond of him. In fact, they are as tired of him as are the factory bosses. One of the most powerful comments on Harry's powerlessness in the novel is that he at one point becomes a bargaining chip in management-union negotiations: the two sides are equally eager to discard him. He, of course, never knows anything about this.

Harry's hubris over his imagined importance as the manager of strike headquarters soon sets in motion the forces of his inevitable destruction; he entices the predatory street gang from the bar across the street to join him at the headquarters. By offering Vinnie, Harry and the boys free beer and food, he is able to guarantee that they will keep him company at night even though they are profoundly contemptuous of him. He desperately needs them so that he has someone to participate with him in the assaultive language of machismo. Moreover Vinnie and the boys are for him, just as they were for Georgette, the very images of male strength and toughness. It is as if Harry believes that being accepted by them will magically negate his secret pursuit of drag queens. The deadly unreality of this belief is underscored by the homosexual acts in which the gang members unapologetically indulge.

LAST EXIT TO BROOKLYN

The motif of deadly masquerade that runs throughout the novel is illustrated in the name of the gay bar, "Marys," where Harry goes to search for scores. The young homosexuals who habituate the bar like Harry well enough but are also more than a little frightened by him:

> Harry was different, or at least they felt he was. There was some little something that they couldnt sense, that they were uncertain about, that eventually made them nervous. It might simply be that Harry would like to dress up as a woman and go to a drag ball, or parade down Broadway; or perhaps some day he would flip and kill one of them. They didnt know. (203)

They are, of course, quite correct to be concerned about him. It is only a matter of time before Harry's always barely suppressed rage and self-loathing will inspire some cataclysmic act of violence.

The inevitable takes place after the strike ends and Harry's position as manager of union strike headquarters is abruptly terminated and after a drag queen named Regina contemptuously rejects him. Now shorn of any illusions about his importance at work and humiliatingly mocked by his surrender to homosexual desire, Harry sets in motion the final act of his destruction. In fact, he seems deliberately to insure that his punishment will be swift and complete. He chooses to mock innocence itself, or at least to come as close to doing so as his fallen world will allow, by making a sexual advance to a young boy. That the innocence of the particular boy he approaches is questionable is an unavoidable reality of the Brooklyn slum.

Harry, responding to his own self-loathing, violates one of the most universal of taboos and thereby assures that his sin will not be forgiven. But in fact another kind of pride is operative here, the kind of twisted and perverted pride of which virtually all of Selby's characters are guilty. Harry chooses not to seek spiritual redemption. That the aesthetic of rage, of a genuine "hatred of God," that dominates *Last Exit to Brooklyn* as well as Selby's next novel, *The Room,* calls into question the possibility of such redemption for anyone does not mitigate against Harry's sin. He quickly receives the harsh punishment that he has sought when the street gang administers to him what surely must rank among the most savage beatings in American or any other literature.

In 1974 Richard A. Wertime published a perceptive, if somewhat overstated, critical analysis of Harry's psychological and symbolic relationship to the street gang. First, Wertime asserts that Harry's brutal punishment is a twentieth-century version of ancient "retributive justice": "retributive justice, at its extreme, engenders a primitive satisfaction: primitive in its unabashed complacency towards violence, primitive in its sensing a serious social endangerment, and primitive in regarding the act of punishment as a manifest social necessity."[16] He then argues that the novel is essentially a study of the landscape of Harry's mind, of his "private psychosis," and that the street-gang members function metaphorically as "psychic avengers," as manifestations of Harry's self-hatred and need for some supreme punishment (153–154). Finally, he provides a nicely condensed summary of the essential conflict driving Selby's psychotic shop steward:

> . . . Harry's sense of deficiency derives from an unreal notion of what he ought to be instead of what he actually is. His conscience has him caught, then, in a double bind: on the one hand it condemns him as being hopelessly inadequate, and on the other hand it orders him to assume, in compensation, an identity which is beyond the power of any man to achieve. (160)

This complex arrogance originating in self-loathing then motivates Harry, beaten virtually beyond recognition and hanging by his arms to a billboard, to mouth silently what he judges to be the ultimate blasphemy of accusing God of committing fellatio. His sin is now complete—unlike Job, he has chosen to curse God and is now ready to die.

In fact, throughout *Last Exit to Brooklyn* the street gang functions on several levels, both symbolic and realistic. They play significant roles in several of the novel's other episodes: for example, the Georgette and Tralala stories and the brief opening segment entitled "Another Day Another Dollar," in which for no reason whatsoever they attack, beat, and nearly kill a young soldier attempting to return to the Brooklyn army base. Since this segment seems to occur during either World War II or the Korean War, the gang members' absence of, in fact their actual contempt for, anything approaching patriotism is emphasized. There is no particular reason, even in this historic period, that they should feel any loyalty to it. As the human detritus of the city, they exist in America but are in no other way a part of the country; present reality is for them meaningless and boring, and they know that they have no real future.

They are the predators of the wasteland of urban America, hating everything and devoted to nothing. Lacking a spiritual component in their personalities, they seek no redemption. After assaulting Harry Black later in the novel, they simply return to the Greeks, the cheap diner out of which they operate, and celebrate the attack;

> The guys washed up in the Greeks, drying their hands with toilet paper and tossing the wet wads at each other, laughing. It was the first real kick since blowing up the trucks [during the strike they blow up some company trucks which are being driven by scabs]. The first good rumble since they dumped the doggy [the attack on the soldier in "Another Day Another Dollar"]. They sprawled at the counter and at the tables and ordered coffee. (228)

In summary, the cumulative character of the street gang plays a complex and important role in *Last Exit to Brooklyn.* As a technical device it links the separate sections of the novel together while working within the narrative on both a mimetic and a symbolic level. Unmistakably "real" as characters, Vinnie and the gang also personify the frustration and raw rage that permeates the world of the inner city.

The novel concludes with a coda called "Landsend" that narrates in almost unbearable detail the crude and senseless fate potentially awaiting the gang members. Landsend is the name of a government-sponsored housing project to which Vinnie, Harry, and Sal will in all probability have to retreat if they live long enough. In this concluding segment Selby depicts a world populated by creatures so warped by cruel selfishness and rage-filled lust that they no longer seem human. Further, he develops an innovative narrative strategy to suggest the relationship of this concluding coda to what has preceded it; names from the earlier sections reappear, but there is no way to be certain that they designate the same individuals that have previously appeared. A significant thematic point is implicit in this narrative innovation—in Landsend no real individuals can be found, only brutalized and brutalizing creatures who merge into a nightmarish composite portrait of hatred and despair.

Just as the street gang emerges as a cumulative characterization of the purposeless, violent youths who roam the streets of Brooklyn, the inhabitants of the housing project personify the sordid middle age awaiting Vinnie and the gang. The brief account of the marriage of Vinnie and Mary in this concluding section captures the essence of the erotic and ultimately sacrilegious sexuality that runs throughout Selby's work.

Compared to Vinnie and Mary, T. S. Eliot's clerk and typist in *The Waste Land* seem almost romantic. The narrative communicates the nonsexual moments in the marriage of Vinnie and Mary almost entirely in capital letters; they are so filled with rage that they cannot talk *to* each other, they can only scream *at* each other.

Yet this pathetic couple is, if only barely, still recognizably human. In contrast there is the distinctly dehumanized group of women whose combined perspective works as a "WOMENS CHORUS" in the novel. At one point they sit outside watching an unattended baby who has crawled onto a window ledge on the fourth floor of the building; they respond to the increasing danger of the baby's situation by loudly cheering for it to fall. When the infant is saved, they feel that they have been let down and yearn "for a little more excitement" (281). In an early study of *Last Exit to Brooklyn,* Charles D. Peavy argues that the novel can be read only as part of a tradition of moral satire that emphasizes the sinfulness and moral degradation of characters through deliberately excessive detail: "[Selby belongs to the tradition of the religious-moralist-satirist that includes Swift and Pope and which began with the medieval preachers who denounced lechery and gluttony by presenting repulsive portraits of the sins of the flesh."[17]

Last Exit to Brooklyn is a text deliberately designed to assault the reader's sensibilities; its dominant aesthetic mode is one of outrage. The novel repeatedly transgresses against the most fundamental and sacred beliefs of the traditional Western reader by suggesting that the very essence of "humanness" may be a fragile artifice doomed in twentieth-century urban civilization. Not only does it introduce such profoundly blasphemous figures as Tralala, Harry Black, and the WOMENS CHORUS to American literature, but it does so with a minimum of narrative mediation to soften their profound rage and alienation. In his first novel Selby perfected a unique point of view, slight variations of which he would also use in his next three novels. *Last Exit to Brooklyn* opens with a third-person omniscient point of view but then periodically and almost imperceptively shifts in and out of something close to a first-person narration.

The reader thus hears the rage-filled voices of Selby's characters with shattering immediacy. Moreover the style changes little throughout the novel; the language of the novel emerges directly from the violent, crude, and profane speech of the urban characters it describes. His friend Gilbert Sorrentino has offered one of the most incisive comments on Selby's aesthetic:

> [Selby] has put all his faith and energy into the composition of works in language that is that of everyday cheapened discourse, and *without calling attention to the fact that he knows better. . . .* He has disappeared into his books, and his books proffer an art made out of trash and garbage. He gives us no commentary, no opinions, no ideas. He gives us—and this is what constitutes his uncanny power—*no comfort.* He "is" the specific vulgarity, cruelty, and madness that relates in a vulgar, cruel, and mad tongue, the vulgarity, cruelty, and madness of his closed world.[18]

This unique aesthetic enables Selby—while simultaneously creating a highly innovative body of fiction in *Last Exit to Brooklyn* and his subsequent work—to complete the naturalistic assault on the genteel tradition in American literature begun by Frank Norris and Stephen Crane in the 1890s. It also gives his work a strikingly prophetic note. Richard Gehr makes the ironic point that, when the film version of Selby's novel was actually shot in the Red Hook section of Brooklyn in 1988, the neighborhood of the novel had become

UNDERSTANDING HUBERT SELBY, JR.

an even more violent and impoverished place. Crack, unemployment and corruption—both public and private—have created a racially divided atmosphere of helplessness, anger and fear whose dimensions [the novel] merely portends. Brooklyn is crumbling fast, and the rest of the country is apparently keeping pace, alas; which is why, in the eyes of many citizens of the Old World, our cities are now perceived as disintegrating Third World enclaves populated by crass masses left dangling by the rich and powerful. (36)

CHAPTER THREE

The Room

At one point early in Selby's second novel, *The Room,* the anonymous, imprisoned central character plays a solitary "game"—lying on his cot, he focuses his eyes upon the bare overhead light in his cell until they begin "to water and smart." Shutting them, he is briefly comforted by his tears gently gliding down his cheek; then he compulsively begins to repeat the action "until his eyes started to pain and then he just closed them and relaxed. . . ." As the pain subsides, he is finally able to sleep, "wrapped in the comforting strength of hate."[1] *The Room,* perhaps even more than Selby's other novels, reveals the ways in which pride and self-loathing, rage at others and hatred for self, misogyny and the revulsion of male characters toward their own bodies are inextricably intertwined for his antiheroes. In this novel as in virtually all of his fiction, these conflicting feelings and emotions constitute sets of mirror images that inevitably mesh into each other. Selby dispenses with a traditional plot in *The Room* in order to illustrate the desperate and terrifying internal landscape of a single human consciousness. As a result it is not always possible to isolate a precise external reality in the novel.

As is customary in Selby, the possessor of this nightmarish consciousness is enraged by his powerlessness and his fundamental insignificance in modern urban society. That he is literally nameless throughout the novel illustrates his social impotence and anonymity. Atypically for a Selby creation, his entrapment has a literal as well as a metaphoric dimension—he is in jail throughout the novel, having been arrested on a charge that is never quite specified in the novel. It is, of course, easy to assume a Kafka influence here, as in Selby's works generally; and the ambiguity surrounding the focal character's arrest is essential to the creation of a surrealistic aesthetic that is, if possible, even more extreme than that found in *The Trial*. Initially, at least, it is difficult to be certain what happens, or indeed if anything happens, outside the generally demented mind of the focal character. Still it is *possible* to assume this much: he was, shortly before the novel opens, arrested by two police officers at night in front of Kramers Jewelry Store. Even assuming this much provides no necessary clue to the man's literal guilt or innocence. By keeping vague the charge on which his character was arrested, Selby opens possibilities ranging from attempted burglary to simple loitering. Whatever the charge, the prisoner is guilty in the way that all of Selby's people are—guilty of the sins of pride and hatred of the self and others.

Such crafted ambiguity is essential to the novel's aesthetic in other ways as well. *The Room* is, in fact, on one level a tour de force, a sustained experiment in narrative indeterminacy. Of Selby's four novels it is the most experimental in technique, the one that most overtly supports Jerome Klinkowitz's assertion that Selby can be seen in retrospect as "the grandfather of experimental realism,"[2] though, arguably, one could better make this claim for Nelson Algren. At times the prisoner seems incapable of anything more threatening than loitering. The psychological damage that he has endured since childhood has transformed him into a man haunted by fear as well as driven by rage; indeed his rage is a reflection of his profound knowledge of his inadequacies as a male and as a human being. His internal prison is made even darker by the fact that, unlike T. S. Eliot's J. Alfred Prufrock, he exhibits no evidence of possessing a cerebral or intellectual dimension. Instead he exemplifies Selby's urban "Everyman," the product of a shallow, repressive, and misogynistic popular culture. *The Room* offers more than ample evidence of Josephine Hendin's thesis that the Selby Everyman is driven by a pathological hatred of the female. In fact, more overtly in this novel than in the rest of his work, Selby investigates the sources and origins of a truly insane level of misogyny; and it is only in the passages devoted to this investigation that the novel seems somewhat dated and simplistic.

The prisoner's general fearfulness and impotence ironically contribute to the cumulative terror of his characterization. Desperately attempting to repress awareness of his powerlessness and insignificance as well as to escape the boredom of existence in his cell, he engages in a series of fantasies, all centered around the desire for revenge against the two police officers who arrested him. The initial fantasy is an obvious borrowing from the mass culture of film and liberal popular fiction and is characterized by deliberately trite and melodramatic writing. From this comparably innocuous beginning the prisoner's imaginings become increasingly savage and brutal, centering around two prolonged "events": his torture and dehumanizing of the two officers and their terrible rape and physical and mental destruction of a woman called Mrs. Haagstromm. The unrelenting and detailed horror of these two "unreal" episodes is nearly unbearable in its intensity and at times

UNDERSTANDING HUBERT SELBY, JR.

almost too horrific to read. According to Selby the level of savagery here is even upsetting to him. In a 1988 interview he says:

> Now, *The Room* was the most disturbing book I have ever read. I mean, it is really a *disturbing* book, Jesus Christ! I didn't read it for twelve years after I wrote it. . . .
>
> Well, there were some times when I was so startled by what came out on the paper, I couldn't believe it. I know I didn't have the right not to put it on the paper.[3]

That the prisoner is even capable of imagining such horrendous levels of cruelty makes it difficult for the reader to believe in, or even remember, his possible literal innocence while reading these surrealistic fantasy sequences. That difficulty is essential to communicating the genuinely shocking nature of Selby's artistic insight—human beings are not only capable of imagining but of enacting the kind of brutality depicted here. The history of the last sixty years has shown that they are capable of much worse. One feels the presence of the Holocaust as an implied subtext in the novel.

It is should also be pointed out that a unique level of irony is operative here, one which highlights the Sade-like eloquence in the prisoner's fantasy of revenge. For as long as he can sustain the two fantasies, not only Mrs. Haagstromm but the two policemen themselves are trapped in the insane prison of his mind, just as he is at least temporarily forced to exist in a suffocating nine foot by six foot cell. As mentioned, Selby's art acquires its unique power from his narrative cultivation of obsession and claustrophobia.

THE ROOM

Selby in a 1992 interview acknowledges an autobiographical dimension to the novel. When asked what constituted "the basis for writing *The Room*" and if it was not true that he had experienced "some time in jail," he neither quite confirms nor denies the assumption underlying the question:

I did spend a couple months in jail, but the basis for *The Room* is variations on a musical theme. You have a theme of the prisoner's reality which includes such variations as his memory of it and his projections. You might call it an enigma variation. I wrote a story in jail called "The Sound" and that is where the concept for the novel started. . . .

The reason I was in jail was for possession of narcotics. Heroin. [The actual charge was driving while under the influence.] The drugs were an extension of all the addictive medication I had when I was in the hospital [during his long and nearly fatal illness].[4]

Despite the novel's origins in Selby's personal experience, the psyche exposed luxuriating in the sadistic dehumanization of the two policemen and in their equally sadistic attack on Mrs. Haagstromm initially seems inhuman, primordial; and this sense of the nonhuman constitutes one important reason to remember that the novel is an artistic artifact with a nonverbal, musical inspiration. Here the novelist is seeking an aesthetic truth that lies buried beneath human rationality.

Selby's most shocking and horrific insight in *The Room* is precisely that such cruel savagery is quite human. In making this point Selby is following in the literary path of Poe, whom he admittedly admires and often echoes,[5] as well as of the turn-of-the-century naturalists, especially Stephen Crane and Frank Norris. Yet the extreme modernist narration utilized by Selby makes *The Room* sometimes seem foreign to the fiction of Poe, Crane, and Norris and indeed to the dominant legacy of American fiction. When Selby asserts in his 1981 interview with John O'Brien that he is a distinctly "'American' writer," O'Brien responds that, while he can accept this self-analysis as being appropriate for *Last Exit to Brooklyn* and *The Demon,* he "wonder[s] about *The Room.*[6]

Remembering that it was expressed more than a decade ago, it is not difficult to understand O'Brien's reservation about the "Americanness" of this unique and disturbing novel. There is something European about the structure and tone of *The Room.* In both form and content it recalls Jean Genet's *Our Lady of the Flowers.* As mentioned earlier, there is always an echo of Genet in Selby's explorations of sexual and social rage and of the extremes of moral and spiritual despair and "depravity." In its remorseless exploration of the human capacity for cruelty to self and others, *The Room,* again like all of Selby's work, is more than a little reminiscent of Céline's *Journey to the End of the Night* and *Death on the Installment Plan.* In his second novel Selby initially foregrounds the legacy of American optimism and idealism only to explicitly mock and deny it at the end. The unnamed prisoner does certainly personify Selby's urban Everyman, but he seems to have nothing in common with Walt Whitman's divine "common man."

Thus Michael Stephens asserts that "the style [of the novel] is quite transparently French à la Existentialism. *Last Exit to*

Brooklyn used violence to portray the energy in the prose, and the place was certainly within America. *The Room,* with its despairing abstractions, seems to be a cubicle from Sartre or Beckett."[7] Stephens's argument makes a great deal of sense; in its dominant vision Selby's fiction, and especially *The Room,* does have more in common with French literary existentialism than with the mainstream of American literature. His characters are always enticed by the darkness of nonexistence, of "Nothingness," and in desperate flight from the ethical challenge of "Being"; their social anonymity and insignificance simultaneously attracts and enrages them through the illusion of making a meaningful choice. While the prisoner in *The Room* longs for escape from the physical restrictions of "the cell in which he was locked yet did not exist" (92–93), he nevertheless feels "a comfort and a sense of power" there (97). The "little 9x6 room" functions as barrier between him and the reality of his impotence and anonymity. Ultimately, though, the nameless man, like other existential characters, cannot escape the trap of consciousness, and even his fantasies betray him.

In its account of the horrific nature of the prisoner's imagination, *The Room* is reminiscent of much European literature inspired by the Nazi experience. As hideous as they are, these fantasies of the torture and degradation of the two police officers and of Mrs. Haagstromm seem almost insignificant in the context of Nazi atrocities—in the torture chamber of the imprisoned man's mind, one encounters, after all, only the *imagined* destruction of three human beings rather than the *real* murder of millions. Selby's importance lies partially in the fact that he, as powerfully as any postwar American writer, has portrayed the brutal legacy of World War II, a legacy to which Americans have hardly been immune. Hendin correctly argues that "Selby's power comes from his ability to manipulate hate, embrace it as a fact, and love it because it is there."[8] The prisoner's two sadistic revenge fantasies illustrate this aesthetic of hate and also evoke a terrifying moral void at the very heart of the postwar world.

Yet it must be said that Selby does not concur with the critical view of the inherent foreignness of *The Room;* "I think that [it] is as American as the others in a far more implicit way. Its undertones." Somewhat perversely, he only clarifies this point in a later comment about the universality of his narrator: "He's Everyman. That's why he's nameless. He's Everyman. He's like the flat area from Texas to the Canadian border. And that's why he has the kind of fantasies he has" (O'Brien, "Interview," 322). This poetic evaluation is intriguing. Selby's implication seems to be that the prisoner's fantasies of torture originate in the fact that he is himself tortured by a peculiarly American kind of emptiness. If so, he is echoing a thematic motif central to earlier twentieth-century American literature; the idea of a peculiarly "American" loneliness has been expressed by Hamlin Garland, Sherwood Anderson, and Sinclair Lewis among others. It should be said that Garland, Anderson (at least in *Winesburg, Ohio*), and Lewis were writing specifically about the cultural barrenness of rural and small-town America. Perhaps Dreiser and Nelson Algren most clearly anticipate Selby's focus upon a distinctly urban American alienation.

Selby's spatial metaphor for American loneliness at first glance seems more appropriate to the fiction of Garland, Anderson, and Lewis than to his own. Yet it can be surmised that in it

THE ROOM

he is utilizing the relative emptiness and flatness of the land in the Midwest to signify the fundamental isolation of the American soul. His construction of an aesthetic that seems more European than American does not negate the validity of his insight into the spiritual alienation imprisoning the American soul.

The difficulty in always being certain of what is "real" in *The Room* originates primarily in Selby's subtle shifting back and forth between first and third person in his narration. In addition the different levels of "reality" on which the novel functions further complicate this difficulty. For brief moments a third-person narrator recounts the prisoner's thoughts and actions when he is in the company of others, especially in the prison mess hall. In these instances he feels especially alone and desperately vulnerable. When in the physical company of others, he is forced to confront his own powerlessness, the fact that he has no real control and is instead literally controlled by others. Thus it is hardly surprising that he is relieved and feels "safe" when these public occasions are over and he can return to the sanctuary of his cell (261). Especially, near the end of the novel when the antihero's fantasies begin to turn on him and he must acknowledge the full measure of his insignificance and anonymity, the third-person narration emphasizes his isolation as he is locked *inside* his cell but *outside* any comforting memories. It is then that he becomes the most profoundly human and deserving of compassion.

On the level of literal unreality the novel depicts not only his fantasies, but a sequence of consistently painful memories. As Selby has pointed out, one can always distinguish between the prisoner's "memory" and his "fantasy:" "You can tell what's

UNDERSTANDING HUBERT SELBY, JR.

fantasy and what's actually memory by checking the rhythms of the line and the language" (O'Brien "Interview," 320). In the memory sequences Selby's technique of shifting almost imperceptively back and forth between first and third person dominate the narration. In these sequences the language and line length are more conventional than in the fantasy passages. In contrast the opening affirmative fantasy uses the trite language and form of American popular culture, while the extended sequences of the imagined torture and dehumanization describing the arresting police officers and the rape and destruction of Mrs. Haagstromm assault the reader with accelerating brutal language and imagery.[9]

The "memory" sequences are, especially in comparison to the rest of the novel, disappointing because they try to "explain" the prisoner in a formula of almost textbook Freudianism. Like all the males in Selby's first three novels, the prisoner hates women. In the words of Hendin, Selby is unique in his ability to express a primal, a "primitive," degree of misogyny: "The relentless pursuit of machismo through all the ways of cruelty, the fear of failure and worthlessness that drives men into deeper and deeper vileness are Selby's preoccupations. He is a clinician of male violence, dissecting straight to the center of sexual chaos and cruelty" (*Vulnerable People,* 59). Hendin's insight is certainly true to a degree, but *The Room* is evidence that the novelist can most accurately be described as "the *poet* of male violence." Selby communicates more powerfully than perhaps any other writer the savage *irrationality* of male hatred of the female; not surprisingly then he is limited in his attempts at a rational explanation of this phenomenon.

It should be said that not all Selby commentators agree with this criticism. Eric Mottram argues that a sweeping social relevance is implicit in Selby's treatment of the prisoner's Oedipal rage: "The book is a modern classic of oedipal fantasies against law, authority and the impersonality of victimizing justice, with the mother functioning as a pillow for tears and comfort for the lying self-righteousness of an infantile son."[10] While it is true that the prisoner remembers his mother as a deceptively dangerous authority figure who suffocated him with a consuming love and protectiveness, the thesis that she can be seen as emblematic of a corrupt and repressive society seems too great a leap.

Besides the mother there are other female figures in the memory sequences, none of whom threaten Selby's antihero in any realistic manner, but whom he nevertheless comes to hate and fear. Most crucially, there is Mary, the partner of his initial adolescent sexual explorations, mutual masturbation in the homes where Mary is babysitting and in movie theaters. Both Mary and the youthful narrator are afraid to go any farther than this. Even so, anticipation of the meetings with Mary and the excitement of her body, as well as the potential danger of their being discovered, almost chokes him. Yet, at home each evening after being with her, he is overtaken by a vague sensation of something lacking or "just not right" in his sexual activity with Mary (129). More than frustration over the absence of actual intercourse, the young boy seems to be feeling for the first (and apparently last time) in his life regret at his inability to feel genuine affection for a female or for that matter for anyone besides himself.

Here, as is consistently true in Selby, sexuality functions as a barrier to any transcendent emotion. Soon, in fact, the boy's actions with Mary cause him to feel guilt and shame. Inevitably for a Selby male he begins to associate the girl's body, and his mother's body and all female bodies, with human materiality and decay: "Like trying to eat that breakfast with [his mother's] smell. It was the same as Marys, and all the others, but different. All her own. . . . All their own stink, and all the same" (121). Overtly in *The Room* and implicitly in his other work, Selby associates Oedipal attraction and adolescent sexual arousal with the male's initial awareness of his mortality.

Sex then for the Selby male is linked with death rather than with birth and life. As mentioned in connection with *Last Exit to Brooklyn,* the obsession of his male characters with anal intercourse signifies this negative association. (Interesting insights into Selby's fiction might well be derived from a feminist approach to his work, especially one based on the Lacan-inspired French feminists.) Their equation of the body with death makes even heterosexual genital intercourse for the anonymous prisoner in *The Room,* as for Harry Black and the street gang in *Last Exit to Brooklyn* and Harry White in *The Demon,* seem ugly and perverse. It is not surprising then that they become obsessed with acts of rage and displaced vengeance against the female. One of the nameless man's childhood memories is of being aroused by a comic-book drawing of "a white woman chained to a pillar in a large hall" and threatened by "an ancient and evil looking oriental" and "you knew he was going to do something horrible [to her]" (130).

Mottram has discussed Selby's implicit critique in this "Fu Manchu" allusion and indeed in much of his writing of "a class, authoritarian society" in which "media responsibility for racist and sexist violence is well-documented" (356). Indeed the comic-book description is classic pre-1960s popular American soft-core pornography: the satanic embodiment of the non-Western male threatening the white female embodiment of national purity with rape and other unspecified savagery. Typically the woman is bound, and her body is partially exposed to the cruel and merciless "Oriental."

Needless to say, for the male suffering from such a psychosis, sex with a woman can never involve love or any transcendent emotion. For the nameless prisoner, as for most of the other male characters in Selby's first three novels, heterosexual desire culminates in a sense of entrapment signified by the female body and by the penis as well. Near the end of the novel the prisoner is humiliated to discover that he has had a sexual discharge while sleeping; perhaps no passage in all of Selby is more crucial to an understanding of the sexual damage suffered by his male characters and their resulting desperation than the one describing this incident.

Sexuality for them means a recognition of their entrapment in the body and thus a "sickening" awareness of loss of control and the inevitability of death. Irrationally they blame the female—beginning with the mother figure—for this painful epiphany and thus hating her, relentlessly seek revenge, luxuriating in prolonged fantasies of rape and other brutal assault. As mentioned in connection with *Last Exit,* despite an elaborate front of machismo, penetration of the vagina becomes for them a degrading immersion into corruption and decay. Selby's first three novels play extreme variations on Hemingway's concept of the masculine fear of being "biologically trapped." It is only in *Requiem for a Dream* and the short-story collection, *Song of the Silent Snow,* that an affirmative responsive to the female, and especially the mother figure, appears in Selby's work.

Even though the other female figures in the prisoner's memories of youth played, in comparison to the mother and Mary, insignificant roles in his life, his memories of them are similarly angry and bitter. The most important inadvertently sets in motion the man's first arrest, at the age of fifteen. The later fantasy of Mrs. Haagstromm is a composite of all the women whom he remembers from childhood and adolescence and most obviously of his mother, Mary, and a nameless young runaway girl. At age fifteen the prisoner ran away from home "again," this time to Providence, where he found a job on an oil barge. Selby, in a metafiction manner, highlights the symbolic significance of his temporary city of refuge: "Providence. Good name. Providence," (77) signaling a revealing, rather than an affirmative, name.

With a fellow barge worker named Tom, the young antihero went into town where they met the runaway girl in a park. Quickly the more aggressive and experienced Tom propositioned her to accompany them behind a small house. After Tom had intercourse with her, the young protagonist followed but, because of fear and sexual ignorance, only kissed and fondled the girl. Nevertheless he and Tom were arrested by two officers almost immediately upon leaving the park and were accused of having raped the girl. During the subsequent police interrogation he silently confirmed his guilt because "He knew it was wrong and his shame made it impossible to know anything" (78). During his incarceration he was relentlessly tortured by thoughts of the likelihood of his mother's probable discovery of his arrest. In the context of the entire novel this episode has a kind of nostalgic feel; it seems almost impossible to imagine that this frightened and innocent fifteen-year-old becomes the prisoner obsessed with fantasizing sadistic dehumanization of Mrs. Haagstromm and the two policemen who have arrested him in the novel's present tense. Yet Selby has masterfully transcribed his character's consciousness to make this transformation seem not only comprehensible, but in fact inevitable.

Specifically referring to Selby's deliberately trite idealistic fantasy of courtroom revenge, John O'Brien writes that "In various parts of the novel one can hear the echoes of Cagney, Bogart, or the Paul Muni of *I Am a Fugitive from a Chain Gang*" and points out that, in recounting his antihero's fantasies, Selby has borrowed extensively from "Hollywood B movies, popular genre fiction, and/or comic books" ("Materials of Art in Selby," 378). In fact, such images from Hollywood and other mass media echo throughout *The Room*. The stereotype of the sadistic adult criminal deeply devoted to his mother will be familiar to anyone who has seen such classic Cagney films as *Public Enemy* and *White Heat*. Selby has simply taken this stereotypical characterization, emphasized its Oedipal nature, and turned it inside out.

At any rate the teenage girl in this episode from the antihero's adolescence is subsumed in the fantasy of Mrs. Haagstromm as the two police officers who arrested and ridiculed him when he was fifteen merge into the two who have arrested him in the novel's present tense. His lingering hatred for the anonymous girl results from his irrationally blaming her for his humiliation by the police and the legal system as well as for the guilt and shame he feels toward his mother. This same kind of irrational blame is central to the prisoner's memories of the other female figures. At age eight, after being forced by other boys into a fight, he was bitten by a dog owned by a woman; later two policemen, who initially appeared to the eight-year-old to be "two huge giants," came to his house to talk to him about having been bitten. He immediately assumes that they have come to arrest him for the fight which he has deliberately kept secret from his mother. In this childhood incident as in the adolescent experience, a largely passive female initiated an action which resulted in his being questioned by a pair of police officers (in both cases the number probably was chosen to echo the popular culture formula of a hero outnumbered "two-to-one"), and his subsequent guilt toward his mother fuels the violent rage of his adult fantasies. It is hardly an accident that, in order to dehumanize the two officers from the novel's present tense, he imagines turning them into dogs. The incidents of the dog biting and the arrest while he was a teenager, of course, support Mottram's argument for a broadly social Oedipal reading.

Three other women whom the arrested man remembers were objectively even more incidental to his childhood and adolescent. He obsessively recalls having been embarrassed by a teacher who asked him a math question; when he did not know the answer, the other students dissolved into laughter. Inevitably for a Selby protagonist, his still intense rage focuses on the teacher and not the laughing students: "Rotten bitch. / There was more than 1

number [as answer to the math question]. I wasnt really wrong"
(233). Like Harry Black of *Last Exit to Brooklyn* and Harry White
of *The Demon,* the anonymous man is entrapped in a large,
relentless, and thus perpetually vulnerable ego; he must always
find someone else to blame for his failures and lack of saving
vision. One hears echoes of T. S. Eliot in Selby's depictions of
individuals tormented by the dual trap of a dominant ego and a
spiritually barren "waste land."

A second woman on whom the antihero obsessively focuses
is little more than a remembered body haunting his suffocating
consciousness. The episode in which she appears recalls the
writing of Hemingway in "A Clean, Well-Lighted Place," as well
as that of Eliot. In it the protagonist remembers once when he sat
behind a young woman in church and imagined, while the
congregation recited the Lord's Prayer, having sex with her. In a
manner comparable to Hemingway's substituting the word *nada*
for important words in the Lord's Prayer, Selby alternates the
biblical lines with an intensely graphic and crude description of
sexual intercourse; like Hemingway, he is utilizing a kind of art-
through-blasphemy to communicate the spiritual barrenness of
his character's existence. But the most passive of all the women
populating his memories is the one who was accidentally shot and
killed by a boy firing from three blocks away at the lights of a
movie marquee. To discover the identity of the shooter, the police
began a search of the neighborhood; and, of course, no more and
no less than two officers came to the young protagonist's room
and "inspected his cap pistol (tom mix) very carefully and
minutely" (76). Inevitably, when recalling this incident, the
prisoner blames the dead woman.

UNDERSTANDING HUBERT SELBY, JR.

Nothing is so revealing of the fundamentally frightened, and even cowardly, nature of the prisoner's misogyny than the fact that in his fantasies he has the two policemen raping and assaulting Mrs. Haagstromm. The composite creation of Mrs. Haagstromm, after all, originates in his mother; and he cannot even on a subconscious level imagine *himself* brutalizing her. But by creating a scene in which police officers destroy her, he can project an image in which agents of the repressive authoritarian social structure victimize a fictional female figure who incorporates all the women he has ever known, beginning with his mother. By fantasizing the victimization of an imminently respectable woman, he can on a conscious level continue to be "appropriate" toward her while indulging in horrific details of her physical and mental destruction. In addition he is able to create a shocking image of the police as sadistic assailants of decent and innocent women.

It is important to remember that the Mrs. Haagstromm fantasy is preceded by the protagonist's melodramatic courtroom fantasy. O'Brien is correct in his perception that the writing in this segment is deliberately trite in order to reflect the manner in which melodramatic popular culture has captured the prisoner's intellect. Reading it, one has no difficulty in detecting echoes of numerous movies of the 1930s and 40s and even the 60s in which an innocent male victim of society, either by himself or with the help of others, is able to defend himself successfully and, in doing so, expose the massive corruption of the American justice system. Thus the reader can play a mental game of film casting while reading this section. In addition to the actors and films mentioned by O'Brien, Henry Fonda in *The Wrong Man* and *The Ox-Bow Incident* and James Stewart in *Call Northside 777* come quickly to mind.

THE ROOM

In his courtroom fantasy the prisoner is aided by a noble and idealistic defense attorney whom he calls Stacey Lowry and a crusading newspaper editor whom he designates as Donald Preston. In actuality he has been assigned an apparently unexceptional public defender named Smith. The fantasy undergoes constant revision as to detail, but its essential focus remains the same, exoneration of the protagonist and subsequent exposure of the corruption in the police department and throughout the legal system, until near the end of the novel. A consistent feature of the details of the sequence is their sheer unbelievability. Initially the prisoner writes a letter to Donald Preston's newspaper on toilet paper with a pencil which he sharpened with his teeth. Later he is not even arrested, subduing the two officers with karate and then phoning Preston with his story.

In the letter from the early version of the incident, the nameless prisoner exposes a massive national conspiracy that has evolved into a "Police State":

> It is time for the people of this State to be awakened to the real and potential danger surrounding them. If something is not done soon to retard the growth of this fascistic cancer we may all be awakened some night to the sound of axes chopping down our doors and Storm Troopers will be dragging us out of our beds [as the two real policemen did to the young boy after the anonymous woman was shot].
>
> I know this to be true as I am one of the victims of this conspiracy. (18)

In a subsequent imaginary conversation with Lowry and Preston, the protagonist significantly comments: "after I went through the ordeal of interrogation and being booked, I started becoming paranoid" (23). Obviously the prisoner has been paranoid for quite some time. Yet it is a paranoia comparable to that elaborated by Norman Mailer in works such as *Advertisements for Myself* and *The Armies of the Night*—it has a genuine basis in contemporary American social reality. Selby's success in examining both the legitimate and the mad levels of the narrator's fears is one of the most impressive aspects of Selby's achievement in *The Room.* Even in such an absurd segment of the novel, one of the protagonist's assertions should not simply be dismissed:

> It was not until I spoke to some of the other inmates, and observed what was happening, that I realized that this was simply an extension and manifestation of a higher, unseen and unheard, authority. Well, I guess I should say unheard except through the lower echelon. (23)

It truly is, Selby believes, economically and politically powerless individuals who most feel the sheer arbitrariness of the American legal system.

Nevertheless the nameless individual is guilty of a moral arrogance and cowardice and an individual selfishness that prevents him, until the end of the novel, from admitting even to himself any responsibility for his life of pain and suffering. In an imaginary press conference he says that he has been charged with "Suspicion. I do not know of what, but they said I was acting suspiciously" (49). Virtually all of Selby's characters are indeed guilty of ethically suspicious behavior, of excessive pride and extreme self-centeredness, characteristics that exacerbate, rather than alleviate, their fear and vulnerability.

For much of the novel Selby's protagonist is able to delay admission of his guilt through his fantasies. The courtroom sequence allows him not only to deny guilt, but to view himself as a hero, supported by the equally heroic but socially prominent and powerful Stacey Lowry and Donald Preston. The sense of powerlessness at the core of the antihero's identity is revealed in his expressed pride when his imagined allies treat him with friendship and equality. (During his "creation" of the actual trial, he refers to Lowry as "Stace.") The deliberate "pop culture" style in this extended segment is so extreme at times as to become almost comic. For instance, there is this passage in which the protagonist proposes to Lowry and Preston that they mount a campaign against all authoritarian evil:

> I think we should make this campaign against all forms of authoritative despotism. What I mean is, there are all forms of abuses of authority—police, politicians, unions, bankers, schools, prisons—and god knows how many others. Also, it seems to me, if you continue a campaign too long people will become immune to it, but with the proper lapse of time between them—and when other news is scarce—you can always go into another aspect of the campaign and expose any one of the authoritative evils in the world.
>
> It is obvious from the manner in which they agreed with him that they not only appreciate his suggestion,

but are aware of the fact that it was not offered because
of any personal vindictiveness. (47)

The comic overtones in the writing disappear when the protagonist begins to imagine the trial not as a forum to expose the two
policemen or any abstract evil authority that they might represent, but as a means to destroy their wives and children. This
sociopathic turn leads inevitably into the novel's two surreal
sequences of sadistic revenge.

To write them, Selby turned to more exotic, if not truly
foreign, sources than those associated with mainstream popular culture. In fact, American hard-core pornography, which
these two extended passages recall, constitutes merely the
dark underside of the popular culture of American films,
television, and advertising. Not surprisingly Selby, in order
to communicate his protagonist's desperate sense of entrapment and outrage, especially echoes pornographic depictions
of bondage and sado-masochism. The imprisoned man is
presently restricted by his "9x6 room" and has always felt
"bound" by his position of social and economic powerlessness.
His psychological pain is excessive and destructive, as is his need
to inflict comparable pain on others.

Again, it also makes sense to read the sequences detailing the
dehumanization of the two policemen and the rape-destruction of
Mrs. Haagstromm in the specific context of post–World War II
and post-Holocaust literature. One implication of the novel is that
since 1945 no human atrocity is unthinkable. Especially given the
obsession with excrement and bodily functions throughout the
novel, these two sequences, and indeed all of *The Room,* can be

interpreted as illustrative of Julia Kristeva's concept of the literature of "abjection," practiced most memorably in French literature by Céline. Kristeva analyzes her revulsion at the sight of a corpse as being the conscious expression of a never-truly-absent awareness of the inevitable collapse of order and "boundaries" that will come with death. For her the most horrific legacy of the Nazis is the utter destruction of the comforting illusion that death is not senseless and arbitrary.

Céline was, of course, in biographical as well as literary terms a perfect subject for Kristeva's discussion of the Nazi role in creating a postwar awareness of abjection. While Selby, in contrast, has never been a Nazi or anything approaching it, one can still legitimately discuss him as one of Kristeva's aesthetic "frontiersmen" of the abject—he relentlessly explores the psychological and physical horror inherent in the boundaries between life and death, the living body and the corpse, the transparency of which boundaries World War II and the Holocaust made horribly clear.

Selby describes his "rage and anger towards God" while writing *Last Exit to Brooklyn* as being a personal thing (Vorda interview, 291); but it seems obvious that he is also expressing through his characters a comparable outrage at living in a postwar world in which all patterns of order and decency have been shattered. Both his first novel and *The Room* can be interpreted in part as probings of the mentality of the incipient fascist—the person who seeks to escape awareness of mortality, as well as social and economic powerlessness, through fantasies of control and violation of others. In fact, in the current context of the emergence in America of right-wing state "militias," *The Room* and especially the protagonist's "letter" revealing the existence of a "Police State" in contemporary America and his two prolonged fantasies of sadism seem to have a renewed relevance.

Ultimately, though, even his fantasies will not permit Selby's desperate antihero to escape. He quickly wrings every conceivable drop of perverse satisfaction out of the two sadism-revenge sequences and mentally returns to his imagined courtroom drama only to lose control of it. Stacey Lowry disappears, and the prisoner becomes his own defense counsel. At the climax of his fantasy he has exposed in true Perry Mason fantasy the two policemen (one inevitably named Harry) through brilliant cross-examination; but near the novel's end he is himself exposed when the judge berates him for violations of proper court procedure and threatens to hold him in "contempt" (279). The word *contempt* functions here on several ironic levels. It implies the impersonal manner in which society has sentenced Selby's protagonist, and indeed all of those trapped in the lower classes, to anonymous, impotent lives. Most crucially, of course, it describes the prisoner's own self-contempt—even in the world of his most secret fantasies, he ultimately judges and condemns himself. In the 1981 interview with John O'Brien, Selby discusses his character's self-judgment:

> The price of hating others is loving yourself less. His self-esteem has gone down. Hate is chewing up any touch of humanity that's left. Underlying his hate is guilt. Sexual, religious guilt, which you see in his fantasies. . . . The tragedy of this man is that he has found *himself* guilty. . . . So, after a while . . . the only source of energy for hate is

oneself. And he is so chewed up with his hate, which comes from his guilt, that he is running out of energy. (322)

This climactic self-condemnation is necessary in order for the reader to accept the final and most significant implication of the novel's central theme. The protagonist's grandiose characterization of himself in the early stages of the courtroom fantasy as the noble and solitary champion of the underdog receives a kind of ironic validation in the last half of the novel. In the mess hall he briefly experiences a moment of silent communion with those around him: "He knew he was the focal point of their despair and frustration. And he knew, too, that though he sat there silently and slowly eating in the midst of the clanging of tin trays and cups that they found the reassurance they needed in his eyes. He was the hope of the hopeless" (96). The vaguely religious tone of this passage and the context in which it appears validate in a highly existentialist manner the protagonist's brief epiphany. In its enforced silence the meal becomes a kind of secular mass or communion in which the other prisoners silently seek, and briefly find, a "holy" figure who will take on the pain and loneliness of their guilt.

While Selby's antihero is still struggling at this point to escape the necessity of self-judgment, this short relief from the prison of his own self-centeredness is crucial to his ultimate emergence as a human being for whom one can feel compassion, rather a monster for whom the only possible feelings are revulsion and fear. Despite the furnace of his raging, savage ego, he has not, in fact, succeeded in "chewing up" all of humanity. As the novel moves to its conclusion, he seeks comfort in the only "friend" he has, his pervasive loneliness. As in the description of the epiphany in the mess room, Selby uses an overtly religious imagery to describe the prisoner embracing his alienation: "He could feel the spirit of his friend flowing through his body, reassuring him, and having finished his journey he returned to his place and nestled deep in his host" (273–74). Tragically, except for brief, unexpected moments he cannot feel communion with others, but only with his own pain and alienation.

The novel can reach conclusion only after the protagonist has made a silent "confession" of the actual pain he has largely inadvertently caused others. He contrasts this "guilt" with the cold, calculated selfishness with which those in control of society treat the lower classes. In a manner again reminiscent of Hemingway, those anonymous figures who control a socio-economic system that results in so much pain for so many are designated as an unknown "they":

Они dont feel flooded by other peoples tears. . . . The dont know what it is to feel the sorrow of the world. . . . Or loneliness. . . . They just sleep and get up and go to work with that same old grin stuck on their face. . . . They just sleep. Unaware and unconcerned. Oblivious to the pain and misery of the world. . . . I didnt plan to hurt anyones feelings. Not like them. They get pleasure out of hurting people. And anyway, I said I was sorry. . . . God, what do you want from me. . . . A thousand and one times I said I was sorry. Isnt that enough. Youd think I was some kind of animal or madman or something. (284–86)

THE ROOM

Finally it is the prisoner himself who withholds absolution. But this final silent confession has affirmed that he is definitely not an "animal or madman," but a human being who despite the extremity of his rage and the brutality of his fantasies must finally be affirmed by the reader as "human. All too human." *The Room* is an uncompromising exploration into the most private recesses of a sick and suffering mind, a mind that is expressive of the most horrible criminal excesses of the twentieth century as well as of the desperate vulnerability of the socio-economic victim. While sometimes echoing the writing of Poe, the American naturalists, and Hemingway, it is a fiction that most clearly recalls the work of such European existentialists as Nietzsche, Kafka, Céline, Sartre, Beckett, and Genet. Whether foreign to the American tradition or not, it is, strictly in terms of fictional structure and control, Selby's best work and in sum the equal of *Last Exit to Brooklyn.*

CHAPTER FOUR

The Demon

In several ways Selby's third novel, *The Demon* (1976), constitutes a significant break with his earlier work. The story of the social and economic rise and more importantly the corresponding spiritual and ethical collapse of Harry White, a successful business executive, the novel follows a conventional linear plot structure. While it is again narrated through Selby's familiar device of shifting occasionally from a dominant third-person perspective to an immediate first-person voice, it avoids the abrupt shifts in narrative time and place that characterize *Last Exit to Brooklyn* and *The Room*. In addition it leaves the economically oppressed world of the earlier novels in order to depict life as lived by the suburban rich. Yet in mood and theme *The Demon* is distinctively and unmistakably the work of Hubert Selby. Unfortunately Selby's attempt in the novel to fictionalize his dark vision while using a conventional fictional structure and an upper-middle-class setting (which was, of course, in itself an experiment) prompted the most consistently negative reviews of his career. Those critics who had always been offended by his work took the occasion of *The Demon*'s appearance to attack not only it, but *Last Exit to Brooklyn* and *The Room* as well. Dean Flower's review in *The New York Times Book Review* was representative of this kind of cumulative assault:

> Hubert Selby's third novel by all odds [is] his most ludi-crous to date. . . . When our hero turns sadist and criminal,

as we know he must—all who succumb to the demon of lust invariably do—the change again fails to surprise. He has simply reverted to type—to the snarling, suffering, sado-masochistic underground man that has always been Selby's real hero. . . . The real moral, however, lies in the obsessive grossness of Selby's style. No wit, irony, qualification, contingency, credibility, subtlety, social or moral complexity appears to distract the monologuist from his dreary exercise.[1]

Of course, this phenomenon is not an unusual one; for instance, those members of the critical establishment who had disliked James Jones's *From Here to Eternity* (1951) but were ignored in the overwhelmingly favorable response to the novel attacked Jones's second, and clearly less successful 1958 novel, *Some Came Running,* with particular and often quite personal venom. Jones and Selby were, in fact, writers whose work was virtually preordained to provoke this kind of extreme response. Each emerged from backgrounds perceived by the critical establishment as being "foreign" to the production and even the consumption of genuine literary and cultural works—Jones the small-town Midwest and Selby working-class Brooklyn. Each wrote in a style that clearly constituted a challenge to modernist symbolism and minimalism. Most crucially, each rebelled against accepted views of literary taste and refinement.

Considerably more sympathetic to Selby than Dean Flower, the *Newsweek* reviewer still questioned the novelist's ability to create convincingly the kind of upper-middle-class world that serves as the setting for *The Demon:* "Selby seems to know little

UNDERSTANDING HUBERT SELBY, JR.

about that sort of life, which far less talented writers invent so easily. Lovely Linda [wife of the protagonist] . . . remains the angelic mannequin one would expect from a writer of Selby's apparently misogynistic frame of mind. Their marriage . . . seems more abstracted than observed."[2] Despite its negative reception *The Demon* is an honest and in many ways successful novel. Though an arbitrary and largely unconvincing ending and some earlier slips into cliché make it undeniably the weakest of Selby's five volumes of fiction, it still represents an important, in fact an inevitable, extension of the central themes that dominated his writing from the beginning. It seems a likely guess that much of the harshness of the novel's reception resulted from an unwillingness on the part of several of Selby's critics and admirers to accept superficially conventional fiction from a supposedly "underground" writer.

The name of the upwardly mobile protagonist in *The Demon,* Harry White, recalls the name Harry Black in *Last Exit to Brooklyn.* Selby seems to be using the two names in order to create the appearance of a set of binary oppositions precisely in order to undercut that appearance. Harry Black is an incompetent, self-destructive blue-collar worker and strike leader; Harry White, in contrast, is something of a genius in his profession, a man of intense competitive drive who achieves great professional and financial success. Thus, as defined by the values of capitalistic materialism, White embodies "the good," and Black "the bad." Yet internally the two characters have a great deal in common; and both are on this level truly representative Selby characters. Each surrenders to internal compulsions that result in intense self-loathing and ultimate destruction.

THE DEMON

In *Last Exit to Brooklyn* Harry Black struggles to resist his fascination with homosexuality and to keep his frightening needs secret from his wife, his coworkers, and most importantly the young men in the street gang, from whom he desperately desires acceptance. Harry White leads a comparable double life. In the first third of *The Demon* he is not as professionally successful as he should be, largely as a result of his obsession with, and regular capitulation to, antisocial and increasingly dangerous behavioral patterns. Initially his need to violate social decorum manifests itself in the seduction of women he does not know but observes and then approaches during his lunch hour. That White always succeeds in his conquests of anonymous and, of course, attractive young women offended more than one reviewer, who dismissed this aspect of the novel as merely the manifestation of macho wish fulfillment on Selby's part. A careful reading, however, leaves no doubt that the novel's implied author understands Harry's obsession with seduction as arising out of intense psychological and spiritual sickness and despair. On one level it is simply a reflection of the competitiveness that pervades every aspect of Harry White and allows him to succeed in business as well as he does.

Yet compulsions considerably darker than the stereotypical competitive urge are involved in his lunch hour seductions. In addition to having youth and beauty the women he chooses must meet one additional requirement—they must be married: "[Married women] were less trouble . . . if they started asking questions about his life or indicated in any way that they wanted to start an 'affair,' he went his merry way."[3] Still, as Harry is aware, the absence of commitment or emotional complication is not the primary attraction of sex with married women for him. Instead it is the "additional thrill" (3) of perhaps getting caught.

Not at all unlike the protagonist in *The Room,* he is internally consumed by guilt and self-loathing originating in his sexuality. As is true of the unnamed prisoner in the earlier novel, it is necessary for Harry White to express contempt for women since their mere presence provokes desire in him, followed almost instantaneously by shame. Though Selby does not overtly explore the subject in *The Demon,* the Oedipal roots of both characters' troubled sexuality could hardly be more obvious. For Harry White women cannot simply be objects of desire; they must also be fantasized agents of punishment.

In explaining to Harry why it has been necessary to pass him over for an important promotion in favor of a clearly less talented man, his boss, Mr. Wentworth, emphasizes that Harry lacks a certain kind of stability and "a clear perspective on life" that can only be gained by marrying and raising a family (78). At the company picnic where the promotion is announced, Harry is introduced to Linda, a young woman whom he has earlier seen wearing a bikini in a swimming pool. On first seeing her he typically feels lust and only lust, perceiving her not so much as a person, but as a collection of provocative body parts. Later though, especially in the light of Wentworth's criticism, it is not at all difficult for him to decide that he is in love with her and must marry her. He does; they quickly have a child, Harry, Jr.; and for a time the Wentworth formula for personal success seems to work perfectly.

Harry rises up the corporate ladder with astonishing speed, amazing even Wentworth with the originality and daring of his corporate strategy. Thus it is not long before he and Linda can move to a luxurious house in the suburbs. Inwardly, though, Harry has not changed; and the obsessive need to endanger himself and all he has through violations of social codes and actual laws exerts itself again. In the 1981 interview with John O'Brien, Selby responded to a question concerning the intensely harsh reviews of *The Demon:*

> in *Last Exit* it's easy enough to "appreciate" the book because it's easy not to identify with those characters. You can say, "That's terrible! What circumstances they were born into! It's a pity! Thank God it's not me!" In *The Room* you're not so sure, but you can still say, "Hell, this guy's in jail." But in *The Demon* there aren't those kind of barriers between the reader and identification with the character. I think that's the big thing: the fear of identification with Harry.

A few lines later he adds, "There's another thing about *The Demon.* I am obviously attacking the American Dream. The old clichés. The very foundations of our nation."[4]

In truth, socio-economic position is the primary way in which Harry White differs from Harry Black and the unnamed protagonist in *The Room;* virtually everything else is superficial, a matter of degrees and circumstances. All three characters suffer from a profound inability to love, which is the ultimate defining fact of their essential selves. Harry Black, inwardly judging and condemning himself as he does so, futilely turns to the gay world for love and support; the prisoner in *The Room* tries to fill this emotional void with hatred of women, of the society that literally imprisons him, and with fantasies of revenge. The psychotic originality of his sadistic fantasies can be seen as the dark and frightening side of Harry White's brilliance and originality in business. White thinks that he likes women, whereas he only desires their bodies and to a large degree only values their bodies as tangible representations of danger and possible punishment.

On a superficial level Harry White has considerably less excuse for his rejection of the promised salvation of love than do the two earlier characters. After all, he does have economic security and even affluence and, more importantly, a wife who loves him. The common critical charge that Linda is a flat, one-dimensional character is largely true, and this flaw in the novel clearly results from Selby's wanting to idealize her and present her as a prototype of the loving woman trapped in a relationship with a selfish and destructive man. Just as he does for his other fiction, Selby includes biblical quotations in the front matter of *The Demon* to guide the reader's thematic understanding of the novel. Here the selection is James 1:12–15:

> Blessed is the man that endureth temptation: for when he is tried, he shall receive the crown of life, which the Lord hath promised to them that love him.
>
> Let no man say when he is tempted, I am tempted of God: for God cannot be tempted with evil, neither tempteth he any man;
>
> But every man is tempted, when he is drawn away of his own lust, and enticed.
>
> Then when lust hath conceived, it bringeth forth sin; and sin, when it is finished, bringeth forth death.

THE DEMON

Harry White gives in not so much to the temptation of lust as to the temptation of that curious combination of self-loathing and arrogance that drives so many of Selby's male characters.

Frantically trying to deny a suffocating inner sense of sinfulness and unworthiness, he becomes intensely and even insanely competitive in virtually every aspect of his life—in his profession, in his lunchtime "conquests," and even in a supposedly friendly game of softball. As with Harry Black and the anonymous prisoner, the desperate nature of his spiritual crisis pushes him toward obsession. For Harry White, giving in to obsession means surrendering to a demon and inexorably to madness. In fact, *The Demon* could be approached as a study of the turn-of-the-century concept of "moral insanity" as redefined through Selby's unique perspective. After Harry becomes bored with seducing married women, his need to defy social norms while exulting in the possibility of being caught and punished manifests itself in theft. Initially it is a small, insignificant theft. But then Henry starts working alone at night in order to steal large business machines from offices located in his own and neighboring buildings, taking absurd risks and again luxuriating in the risk of being caught, while reassuring himself that it was not "really stealing" because "the machines belong[ed] to large corporations and were insured and no one really was hurt by their loss, if they were in fact lost. They were probably found the next day and returned" (253–54).

It is probably safe to assume that Selby would not shed any more tears over corporation losses than his protagonist does. What *is* important here is the arrogant self-centeredness of Harry White's moral vision. How *he* feels is truly the only important thing. Yet his arrogance is inextricably tied to a pervasive self-hatred. Inevitably theft becomes insufficient to satisfy his demonic needs; and he turns to murder, the ultimate control over another, the ultimate risk to self. Now his arrogance has gone as far as it can; his moral insanity is complete. A brief epigram precedes the novel: "A man obsessed is a man possessed by a demon."

The demon that possesses Harry White is essentially a variation of that which dominates and controls Harry Black and the prisoner in *The Room:* a complex, even contradictory, mix of selfish arrogance masking guilt and self-loathing; sexual compulsion thinly (if at all) disguising hatred of the female; and a desire for some form of cosmic judgement and punishment. Harry White no more personifies "the good" than Harry Black can be dismissed as "the bad": rather they personify the literary tradition of the doppelgänger. Except for superficial external differences they are two sides of the same character. It is interesting that, of the protagonists in Selby's first three novels, only Harry White, the successful and respectable one, actually murders anyone. A further twist of irony is that he gets away with the first two murders in part because of his social position.

However uncomfortable he may have been with an upper-class setting, Selby had to write *The Demon* in order to clarify and extend his central aesthetic vision. An exchange with John O'Brien in the 1981 interview illustrates this point:

> [O'Brien:] In a sense, what you did in *The Demon* was to hand out paychecks to the characters from *Last Exit.*
> [Selby:] Cleaned them up a little.
> [O'Brien:] But having money doesn't help them. You give

> Harry all the money that he will ever need, but it's no help.
> [Selby:] He has everything. Everybody in this country has
> the idea that if you have what Harry has, you have it made.
> He's got an estate in Westchester. He has everything. No,
> it's an inside job. He's destroyed from within. (329)

Traditional naturalistic social protest is clearly irrelevant to *The
Demon*—Harry White is hardly a victim of social and/or economic injustice. He is rather the victim of a kind of madness that
Selby believes permeates every socio-economic level of American society; *The Demon* constitutes a unique variation on the
absurdist naturalism that began clearly to emerge in mid-twenti-
eth-century American fiction.[5]

Selby believes that in a deeply ethical and spiritual way all
of American society is mad. He sounds the same warning
throughout all of his fiction—the American male's devotion to
the relentless competitiveness and materialism of capitalism, his
contempt for women and for life itself, and his flight from love
and redemption have corrupted and destroyed the very soul of
American society. The narrator has himself provided the most
convincing analysis of the fundamental symptom of this madness
in Harry White:

> Harry's real problem is separation. That's the basic prob-
> lem. That's what obsessions do. No matter where Harry
> goes, there's the feeling of separation. Although he really
> believes that he loves his wife and his children, there's
> going to be a feeling of separation. That same feeling
> exists, I'm sure, between him and everything and everyone

else in the novel. You can see that separation in all his
relationships, whether it's work, the house, his automobile,
his family. (O'Brien interview, 329)

Harry clearly is so entrapped by a demented self that he
seems unaware of those around him except as they might
gratify his conflicting needs for capitalistic success and
deferred punishment. He is able to function not only normally, but quite successfully, as long as he does for two
essential reasons. "The demon" that possesses him instinctively knows that Harry must appear "normal" long enough
for his soul to be driven completely mad; and his madness is,
after all, distinctive from that of the rest of society only in its
extremity. *The Demon,* like the rest of Selby's fiction, recalls
a number of other writers, quite diverse in their dominant
aesthetic. For instance, the idea of the normal-appearing
madman owes much to Poe, whose work Selby deliberately
echoes more than once. Harry White's final blasphemous
demand for divine retribution recalls both Nathaniel Hawthorne
and Herman Melville.[6] Céline, with his vision of the innate
"crumminess" of the human being, obviously contributed to
Selby's absurdist naturalism.

That Freudian psychology underlies Selby's fiction is
obvious, and, as mentioned earlier, an extensive analysis of
it in the context of the writings of Michel Foucault would be
profitable. Cumulatively Selby's work demonstrates the degree to which oppressive capitalistic structures dominate and
control every aspect of American life—women are almost
always commodified in his four novels. In an early scene in

THE DEMON

The Demon, Wentworth, the boss who will soon urge Harry to get married in order to gain "a clear perspective on life," rewards the protagonist for his good work on an account by accompanying him and two attractive young women to an exclusive hotel room for the night: "The next morning Wentworth was pretty much the corporate executive as he paid the girls, in cash, and checked his pockets to be certain he was not leaving anything behind" (55).

Harry can barely remember what his anonymous "conquests" look like; and in one bit of dialogue Linda unwittingly reveals the degree to which she is depersonalized in her marriage to Harry: "You know something, Mr. White . . . you make me feel lovely. Im just a mirror" (167). Harry's madness reduces everyone around him to a surface designed to reflect the frightening arrogance of his disguised and insane inner being. In fact, he cannot summon any genuine feeling for anyone, even Linda and their children (in addition to Harry, Jr,. they have a daughter who is inevitably named Mary).

Realizing his inability to care, Harry desperately tries to find some substitute for a sustaining human emotion. When he is no longer able to deny the emptiness of his marriage and even of fatherhood, he begins to collect exotic plants:

Harry had to get up earlier and earlier, as the collection of plants increased, so he could check each one and make certain everything was all right and see to it that they got the proper amount of light and water; and mist them so their air would be humid enough. And on the train he read his books [about plants] along with the *Wall Street Journal.* (189)

Inevitably Harry turns a hobby into a kind of unfocused competition—he becomes obsessed with having more, as well as better cared for, plants than anyone else possibly could. That Harry cares only about growing plants indoors illustrates the degree of his essential separation from nature itself. He cannot be in nature; rather he must attempt to possess and control it. Selby's symbolism in having him read books on tending plants along with the *Wall Street Journal,* the "bible of capitalism," should not be overlooked.

Yet no form of "possession" can satisfy his obsessiveness for long, and each manifestation of his demonic need quickly loses its attraction and becomes a taunting reminder of his self-loathing. He soon feels only revulsion for the plants and allows all of them to wither and die. Ultimately it is death that Harry seeks for himself: death as the extreme punishment for his transgressions; death as the ultimate separation from nature, love, and life itself; and death as the only escape from "the demon" of obsession.

After he and Linda return from a weekend vacation in Jamaica during which he felt suffocated while lying on a beach by all the bikini-clad female bodies surrounding him, he returns to New York and reenters "the pit." He finds "a thirsty lush," buys a bottle of whiskey, and goes with the woman to "her sour, roach-infested room" (211). She falls asleep after intercourse, but Harry lies awake engulfed in hatred and self-loathing:

> In the dim light that just managed to penetrate the soot on the window overlooking the air shaft he looked at the thing,

> whatever or whomever it was, next to him. . . . She looked
> and smelled like something that had been left on the beach
> . . . by the receding ocean and was already starting to rot in
> the heat of the tropical sun. (211–12)

Now he has mentally transformed sex into a real obscenity—the abjection of death.

Gilbert Sorrentino has brilliantly analyzed the profound dichotomy between Harry's "speech" and his "interior language." Harry speaks, he argues, in the "clichéd . . . banter" of the American businessman: "the automatic speech of men whose intellectual sustenance derives from profit. [Such speech] is . . . discreetly, even puritanically wary of sex." In contrast, his "interior language . . . is that of madness: foul, profane, murderous. Harry White's articulations show forth the materialist zombie; his inner voice is that of the void."[7] Inevitably Harry discovers murder to be the act that for a time can fill the void at the core of his being. Murder constitutes, of course, the ultimate possession of another human being.

His discovery of murder as a mode of fulfillment comes unexpectedly and only after he is first drawn toward suicide. Standing on a subway platform, he is attracted to, and then obsessed by, the blinding light of an oncoming train. Momentarily he is tempted to throw himself in front of the train: "he knew he was going to leap in front of it, that he could not stop himself, and it felt right, it felt good, it felt exciting, his whole body trembling and screaming as the train roared closer and closer and he leaned further and further over the edge of the platform and the train shot past him . . . " (260). Later, on the train, an exhilarated Harry knows that he has discovered "the answer of answers" (261).

It is not long before the real meaning of the subway experience becomes clear to him—murder rather than suicide seems the
surest way to fill the void within his soul. Unfortunately this new
awareness of Harry's is the beginning of the descent into triteness
that mars the latter part of the novel:

> And with this new consciousness came the pleasure of
> being able to make a game out of it. At least for now.
> Someday the killing would have to be a reality, but for now
> just the contemplation of it exalted him. . . . Nurture, pet and
> caress the anticipation. That was the thing to do. And he
> would. He would tantalize himself just as long as possible.
> Someday the act would be a part of history, but now he
> would just dangle it in front of himself. He could create his
> own suspense. And master it. (262–63)

For once, the novelist's fondness for having his characters think
in the language of American popular culture gets him in trouble
here; echoes of speeches by mad scientists and sadistic
supervillains in melodramatic and low-budget American films of
the 1930s and 1940s are obvious in this passage. It is not at all
difficult to imagine Boris Karloff, Bela Lugosi, or Basil Rathbone
mentally caressing a future act of murder that would become "a
part of history."

Such narrative triteness continues as Harry plans his murder.
He rather quickly decides that his victim must be a stranger if he
is to escape punishment for the crime. Moreover it should be
someone whose life is meaningless and insignificant. After

returning to the subway platform, he has no difficulty in discovering an abundance of possibilities:

> He looked at all the dreary and harried faces on the subway platform. What could life possibly hold for them? Wearing tattered clothes. Ripped shoes. Grease-rimmed shirts and blouses. They probably lived in some roach-infested trap. They obviously did not live, they merely and barely existed. They had forgotten how to smile. If, indeed, they ever knew. He would be doing them and the world a service. (267)

As well as any other passage, this one illustrates the sincere, but flawed and ultimately frustrating, nature of the last forty to fifty pages of *The Demon*. For one thing it is too overtly literary—the lines about the people on the platform not really living and having forgotten how to smile seem intended to echo a body of Western writing, inspired by Dostoyevsky and Nietzsche, centered around the concept of the amoral superman. The style, though, is more reminiscent of treatments of this concept in American popular culture; one thinks, for instance, of two successful film dramatizations of the Leopold-Loeb case, Alfred Hitchcock's *Rope* (1948) and its 1959 successor *Compulsion.*

Yet it should be said that by emphasizing the "tattered clothes" and "ripped shoes" of the crowd Selby convincingly echoes the mentality and morality of the American businessman who judges everyone and everything on a strictly materialistic basis. Similarly the reference to the "dreary and harried faces" of the crowd evokes effectively the desperately boring and insecure lives of those struggling to survive in the urban capitalistic jungle. In expressing compassion for such people, Selby, of course, joins a number of important twentieth-century American writers, Arthur Miller and Saul Bellow being two of the most notable. Moreover it should be emphasized that the description of Harry's pushing a strange man off the platform and in front of a speeding train and the aftermath of that act is anything but trite; it is, in fact, one of the most horrific and unforgettable moments in all of his work.

In keeping with the thematic emphasis of the novel, Harry is for a short time after the murder a better, more exciting lover than he has ever been before. Selby leaves no doubt that this improvement is an unexpected benefit of the murder, of taking "the game" to a new level of risk: "He felt and experienced each and every move with heightened sensitivity and pleasure that were magnified by the sensation of fear, a fear of infinite power, a fear that forced him on and on long after desire had melted and flowed from his body" (272). Sex, power, and death constitute for Harry a desperate and deadly trinity of desires.

In a perverse and ironic manner, Harry begins to comprehend the pain of his isolation, his separation from the world; when planning a second murder, he realizes what was lacking in the first: "Not enough personal involvement. There had to be more personal contact. Yes, that was the solution. He had to be personally involved. More *completely* involved" (276). Thus he decides that the risk factor must be intensified even further. The kind of "personal contact" he desires is monstrous and insane; he decides again to murder a stranger, but this time by stabbing him with a knife in a crowded Times Square. In such a setting the possibility of Harry's being seen and captured would seem great; but it is another of Selby's ironies that the size of the crowd furnishes him a protective anonymity and, his act completely undetected, he escapes easily.

Not long after the second murder, Harry realizes that killing anonymous men is not enough to bring down upon himself the kind of biblical and cosmic judgment that his arrogance and self-loathing demand. For such total condemnation he must commit the ultimate blasphemy of assailing God, of murdering divinity itself; and the pervasive American mass media soon provides him with a means of doing so, at least symbolically. On Palm Sunday a televised "Special Report" shocks him into total and rapt consciousness with images of a large crowd paying tribute to a Catholic cardinal whom the announcer describes as being one whose unique status as modern holy man and prophet is accepted by people from virtually every major religious creed and denomination. Next Harry sees Cardinal Leterman (the man who embodies the letter or literalness of God's existence?) announcing that he will serve Communion on Easter Sunday in Saint Patrick's Cathedral.

The holy man also reminds the assembled crowd, as well as his television audience, that "just sixty-four days ago I was stricken with a heart attack and was rushed to the hospital where I was pronounced dead on arrival . . . yes . . . dead! Yet today I am alive through the grace of God and the ministrations of the dedicated and devoted men of medicine" (294). To the degree that Selby intends all this as a satire of the power of television and other forms of mass media to create not only heroes, but even new manifestations of the divine, one can detect some witty irreverent commentary here. The context of this concluding segment of the novel indicates though that the Cardinal Leterman creation is largely intended to be serious; and, if that is true, the power of the novel is again weakened by cliché. The debt of the Leterman characterization to Dostoyevsky and especially to Nietzsche could hardly be more obvious, a factor that, like so much else in the novelist's work, emphasizes the essentially European and existentialist nature of his aesthetic.

In order to make his condemnation as universal as possible, Harry decides that he must stab Leterman during the Communion service, which will be "televised all over the world" (305). Clichés abound in Selby's description of the murder itself; as a result it is not nearly as shocking as the passage recounting the death of the unknown man whom Harry pushes in front of the subway train. For instance, as he is stabbed, "the beloved Cardinal stood erect with his arms outstretched his shadow forming a large cross. . . . the Cardinals blood flowed forth splattering the fallen Hosts . . . [and then] Cardinal Leterman slowly fell back onto a crosslike shadow like a crucified Christ . . . the eyes of the resurrected man of God continued to look up . . ." (308–09). Selby does provide one original and thematically significant detail: Harry, after being pushed by the shocked and uncomprehending crowd through a side door of the church, is horrified to discover the "god-awful sticky semen wetness" inside his pants" (310). The narrative stresses once again how fundamentally Harry's spiritual sickness is tied to his perverted sexuality.

THE DEMON

The religious overtones so central to the novel's dominant vision are emphasized in a crucial passage describing Harry's hesitation before entering the cathedral to kill Leterman. Assaulted by "the hounds of hell" who begin to "devour" him, Harry knows that his only salvation is from "the hounds of heaven," who stand waiting for him to call upon them: "they waited and waited for the word, hearing the anguish of Harry White as he was being devoured and hoping that his pain and suffering had been enough so he would scream out for help but the hounds of hell came closer and splattered them again with the mutilated flesh of Harry White . . ." (303). The central irony of this passage is that Harry, like virtually everyone in Selby's savage wasteland, waits to hear "the word" that might redeem him. But, again like Selby's other creations, he is too entrapped in his own paradoxical blend of arrogance and self-loathing to hear the saving word of "love." In a 1988 interview Selby responded simply and directly to the question of why Harry doesn't call in the hounds of heaven: "He couldn't hear them."[8] Never hearing them, he commits suicide at the novel's end, embracing at last the ultimate existential punishment of death for which he has yearned and from which he has fled for so long.

Selby goes to some pains to insure against a simple Freudian reading of *The Demon*. He even has Harry see a therapist who talks to him about subconscious conflict, repression of incidents from childhood, and sublimation. The writing in these scenes is so overtly exaggerated that satire of Freudian therapy clearly seems their intent. As the introductory quotation from the Book of James and the biblical allusions scattered throughout it indicate, the novel carries an unmistakably religious message. Flawed though it is, especially in its concluding segment, *The Demon* remains a powerful novel. It is moreover essential to the full expression of Selby's vision of modern American society as being at every economic level a spiritual wasteland driven mad by rage and self-hatred.

CHAPTER FIVE

Requiem for a Dream

Even more than he had *The Demon,* Paul Metcalf condemned Selby's 1978 novel, *Requiem for a Dream,* as a disappointing departure from the narrative experimentation of *Last Exit to Brooklyn* and *The Room.* He judges the generally traditional form of *Requiem for a Dream,* still the most recent Selby novel, as representing a capitulation to the marketplace: "by the time we get to *Requiem for a Dream,* what we have is a competent, 'shocking' commercial novel. Selby skillfully trading on Selby."[1] This rather harsh dismissal of Selby by an old admirer is illustrative of a kind of trap awaiting the "underground" writer—any attempt to reach out to a wider audience may be seen as a kind of artistic betrayal, a selling out. Of course such writers rarely become truly popular with the American reading public—it seems safe to assume, for instance, that Selby's novels will never reach the audience that regularly reads the work of Stephen King, for instance. While *Requiem for a Dream* is in form and structure the most traditional of Selby's novels, further levels of irony are implicit in Metcalf's attack on it as being merely "commercial."

To a degree it recalls the naturalistic protest fiction of the 1930s and later. Since Selby intends it in part as an exposé of a specific social evil, a degree of shock effect is essential to its success, as well as to an appeal to a wider audience than that which normally responds to "experimental" fiction. The most obvious target of Selby's protest in *Requiem for a Dream* is the

UNDERSTANDING HUBERT SELBY, JR.

American drug culture; the novel is intended in part as a warning that the illegal drug trade has the potential to destroy the very fabric of American society. In his 1992 interview with Selby, Allan Vorda discusses with Selby the continuing relevance of his novel: "it seems even more prophetic ten years after it was written with so many people addicted to crack cocaine and the subsequent effect on society in terms of addiction, crime, and violence."[2] Vorda's point is well taken. Just as *The Room*'s evocation of embittered and powerless men trapped in America's lower classes and turning increasingly to violence as a mode of protest seems especially prophetic for the 1990s, so does Selby's dramatization in *Requiem for a Dream* of the sordid and brutal narcotics traffic that is so powerfully entrenched in urban America.

Yet the drug traffic is only a kind of metaphor for the real target of attack in Selby's 1978 novel. He is presenting a nightmarish vision of America as a society that induces addiction in its citizens in order to assert complete control over them. In fact, it is difficult to think of a more frightening depiction of the prison house of addiction in American literature than *Requiem for a Dream*. In it the various ways in which American capitalistic culture plays upon the resentment and loneliness of vulnerable people by promising them new identities is illustrated in grim and relentless detail. Here, even more overtly than in the earlier novels, American capitalism is viewed as a monolith that visibly and invisibly entraps and destroys its citizens. Thus *Requiem for a Dream* is ultimately no more a "drug novel" than is Nelson Algren's *The Man with the Golden Arm* (1949).

Just as Julia Kristeva's ideas concerning the literary exploration of "abjection" can profitably be applied to *Last Exit to*

REQUIEM FOR A DREAM

Brooklyn and *The Room,* Michel Foucault's analysis in *Discipline and Punish* of modern French society as modeled upon the prison could potentially be useful as a means of approaching *Requiem for a Dream.* The structures of Selby's New York are unmistakably entrapping and destructive of privacy. Yet in contrast to *The Room,* Selby's fourth novel is clearly and unmistakably American in idiom, structure, and vision. The sense of a peculiarly American kind of spiritual emptiness that Selby described as underlying *The Room* seems considerably more relevant to *Requiem for a Dream;* the protagonist of *The Room* is "like the flat area from Texas to the Canadian border. And that's why he has the kind of fantasies he has."[3] Harry, Tyrone C. Love, Marion, and Sara Goldfarb, its four central characters, are indeed tortured by a profound ache and loneliness in the very centers of their being and turn to dreams to fill the void; inexorably they become addicted to their dreams which destroy them.

In the interview with Vorda, Selby emphasizes that the origin of their dreams is as uniquely American as is the source of their loneliness:

> We are all dealing with mental obsessions and, in this case, the Great American Dream: if you make it on the outside then everything is going to be fine. It's not true. I don't care how limited or how infinite your dream may be. Success is an inside job because life is an inside job. (Perhaps I'm too involved with America, but it seems like we are more involved with facade than any other country because the influences of Madison Avenue and Hollywood are so persuasive and so powerful.) (301)

UNDERSTANDING HUBERT SELBY, JR.

This conceptual emphasis on "America" necessitated that Selby draw his characters from a wider social spectrum than he had in his first three novels. Marion's origins are upper middle class if not higher, while Sara Goldfarb and her son Harry originally belong to the respectable middle class. The social background of African-American Tyrone C. Love is left rather vague; but, because of his long-standing friendship with Harry, one can probably assume a middle-class background for him as well.

Thus the four main characters cumulatively represent a new direction for Selby's fiction—*Requiem for a Dream* is, in fact, his first novel about the middle class. It is probable that Selby chooses this particular focus not to cloud his emphasis that the pain of Harry, Marion, Tyrone, and Sara Goldfarb originates in an inner spiritual barrenness rather than in economic exploitation. As one would expect of a Selby character, the three young people in the novel are guilty of self-centeredness and pride. Selby brilliantly documents the way in which Harry, Marion, and Tyrone, because of their addictions to heroin, increasingly come to choose self-gratification over concern for each other and for anyone else. Only one critical essay focusing exclusively on *Requiem for a Dream* has thus far appeared; in it, Kenneth John Atchity emphasizes precisely this aspect of the novel: "The alternatives, Selby shows, are love and isolation: there is nothing but delusion in between. Community is based on the vision of love, not on self-serving fantasy."[4] Harry, Marion, and Tyrone initially form a kind of small integrated community, but their addictions result in their ultimately betraying each other. Harry's mother,

REQUIEM FOR A DREAM

Sara, is more clearly a victim than the three young characters; she is to a large degree destroyed by her innocence. Yet in the final analysis she too can be said to have committed herself to a destructive fantasy of egotistic fulfillment.

Despite the self-centeredness of these four vulnerable individuals, they emerge as the most traditionally sympathetic of all the characters in Selby's four novels because ties of genuine love and devotion do initially exist among them. In this way *Requiem for a Dream* anticipates his 1986 short story collection, *Song of the Silent Snow,* in which Selby overtly embraces and forgives most of his lonely and suffering creations. Though the dominant imagery in a crucial early scene in the novel signals that the affair between Harry and Marion is doomed (they initially declare their love while in a morgue at night), its origins nevertheless echo the conventions of Western romantic love. Similarly the bond between Harry and Tyrone is also real, recalling the many instances of deep male friendship in American fiction. Despite his repeated violations of her trust and indeed her property, Sara clearly loves her son. It is essential that these positive feelings be established early in the novel so that their disintegration will induce feelings of genuine regret in the reader.

Their legitimacy is further crucial to the novel's analysis of addiction. Selby illustrates the destructive potential of drug dependency by depicting in a graphic and uncompromising manner the ways in which Harry, Marion, and Tyrone inexorably betray their feelings for each other. In a 1981 essay Selby's friend Gilbert Sorrentino praised the honesty and freshness of this aspect of the novel:

Requiem for a Dream engages the world of drug addiction without resort to sentimentality or romance, and without even a hint of the "outsider" pride that seems to cleave to so much fiction dealing with this material. It can be argued, in fact, that the sentimentality, romance, and perverse pride in the "calling" of heroin addiction, when indulged in by the characters (not the author) accelerates their destruction.[5]

Sorrentino's point is well taken; *Requiem for a Dream* again recalls Nelson Algren's *The Man with the Golden Arm* in its determination to depict the underground urban drug culture as anything but exciting and glamorous. Like Algren, Selby depicts a savage, cold (in one especially memorable scene, *literally* cold) world in which senseless and anonymous death lies in wait at each and every corner.

Sorrentino is also correct in pointing out that Harry, Tyrone, and Marion romanticize the drug world and convince themselves that they can conquer it: "We could double our money. Easy. . . . We wont get strung out and blow it. We/d be cool and take care a business and in no time we/d get a pound of pure and jest sit back and count the bread."[6] As the novel progresses, the concept of a "pound of pure" broadens until it is not only a term signifying a concrete, measurable amount of heroin, but a metaphor or signification of an abstract ideal of happiness. Harry and Tyrone, as well as Marion and Sara, want to acquire a "pure" (tangible, indestructible, and thus unobtainable) degree of happiness and peace. They lie to themselves that such a goal is possible; and the surrounding capitalist society encourages their lies.

The capacity for self-deception shared by Harry, Tyrone, and Marion is especially well dramatized in a jail scene and its immediate aftermath. Approximately halfway through the novel Tyrone is picked up with heroin in his pocket by two narcotics officers who allow him to keep the drugs but extort money from him and arrest him for "consorting" (170). The young black man understands the procedure intuitively—by submitting quietly to the arrest, he is certain to be released as soon as someone comes to bail him out. While awaiting Harry's arrival, he begins to listen to the colorful stories and sayings of "an old time dope fiend, who looked like he was a hundred and four" (170–71). The pathetic old man, "who sat like a guru in the corner dispensing his stories of glory and enlightened wisdom" (173), in fact entertains everyone else in the lockup. He describes his brief stays in several jails and prisons throughout the country and recalls a vanished golden age of drugs so pure and powerful that one did not even have to inject them to get high, a time when marijuana grew wild in public lots and people gathered to inhale whenever the papers announced the "burning" of such a lot.

The longtime addict then assures his listeners that they can survive and even be successful in the drug culture: "Like I said, its not easy to make it in this world, but ya can do it. I know because Im making it" (175). His listeners, including Tyrone, naturally find this proclamation amusing, coming as it does from a man whose body has been virtually wasted away by his addiction and who has just described a lifetime of imprisonment. Not deterred by the reaction of his audience, the dissipated old man outlines a quick formula for success: ". . . stay to the petty thefts. No felonies" (176) and never get involved with a woman.

Suddenly, in the midst of the old-timer's monologue, Tyrone notices that the others are not only laughing, but are paying some degree of serious attention to what they are hearing. In turn this sudden insight almost forces the young black man to the even more painful realization of a "sense of identification," of "something in common" with the man in the cell (176). But Tyrone denies what would be an unbearable admission—that he is a younger version of the "old time dope fiend" and someday may well find himself trapped in a ravaged body and in a jail cell boring his listeners with tales of the old days and with ridiculous advice. In fact, he will experience an even worse fate; at the end of the novel he is trapped on a southern chain gang commanded by a sadistic and racist white man.

Upon hearing Tyrone's story of the old addict, Harry and Marion react in a comparable manner. Harry is further tormented by a fleeting shock of recognition with the pathetic figure but with the help of Marion is able to subdue it. Marion, the intellectual, uses her knowledge of Freudian psychology to deny the warning represented by the old man: "Hes so obviously Freudian that its pathetic. I mean that business about women. Probably impotent. . . . So he becomes an addict. Obvious. Really pathetic" (179). It will not be long until Marion's addiction will destroy her capacity to love Harry or anyone else. Not only will she lose any interest in sex, she will come to regard her body exclusively as a means of obtaining heroin; she will prostitute herself and acquiesce in the commodification of her body.

Marion first sells herself to her psychiatrist Arnold only after Harry encourages her to do so; even then Harry undergoes genuine anguish while waiting for her to return from the assignation. He becomes physically sick to the point of vomiting and then, curled into a fetal position, tries unsuccessfully to vanish into the images of a flicking television screen. When Marion does return, Harry is unable to make love to her; thus the young male addict, rather than the old-timer, suffers from impotence. Yet he persists in romanticizing the drug culture, luxuriating in images of himself as a wealthy and successful dealer.

In a scene that in its obvious unreality is reminiscent of the legal fantasy in *The Room,* he imagines himself making a last pickup at Kennedy airport, a transaction that will enable him to leave the streets behind forever. In his fantasy he and Marion have already realized a shared dream of owning a combination coffee house and small theater in San Francisco and have made plans for extensive world traveling. Despite its otherwise conventional structure, *Requiem for a Dream* also recalls *The Room* in its rapid and subtle alternations of first- and third-person narrative voices. Moreover the parts of the novel that focus exclusively on Harry and Tyrone are told through an experimental narrative voice that echoes the street idiom spoken by both characters. Because the novel shifts with no warning into Harry's fantasy of success, the reader for a moment is seduced into initially accepting it as real. Quickly though, this illusion is shattered by the unbelievable details of Harry and Marion's life of luxury. They have indeed found the mythical "pound of pure." In this fantasy sequence Harry is depicted as still deluding himself about the deadly traps of life in the drug culture; he will die an agonizing death after his arm becomes infected with gangrene, the result of frequent and careless use of the needle.

UNDERSTANDING HUBERT SELBY, JR.

To foreshadow *Requiem*'s tragic ending, Selby incorporates a quite different kind of scene later in the novel, one that is as brutally horrifying as anything in his earlier work. It is winter and warfare in the upper echelons of organized crime has resulted in a "panic," or controlled heroin shortage, in New York; and the desperation of the city's addicts has turned its mean streets into a frozen war zone:

> All the neighborhood streets were filled with dope fiends, even in the snow and sleet, looking for something, anything. Every hallway was cluttered with sick faces with runny noses and bodies shivering with the cold and junk sickness, the cold cracking the marrow of their bones as they broke out in sweats from time to time. . . . When someone did cop he then had to make it safely to his pad, or some place, where he could get off without someone breaking down the door and stealing his dope and maybe getting killed, or killing, if he didnt want to part with something more precious, at that particular moment, than his life. . . . (189)

Ultimately such an extreme "panic" is too dangerous to be maintained; and the city officials, including the police, and the chiefs of the drug trade declare part of the city a "demilitarized zone" in which a limited amount of heroin will be sold openly. Fully aware of what they are risking, Harry and Tyrone enter this zone of death in order to make a purchase; and, despite the horror surrounding them, they continue to believe and to tell themselves that they are not really addicts like the others waiting in line with them: "Harry and Tyrone dug those dudes and shook their heads, knowing they would never get that bad, that they would never get strung out and live just for shit" (220). The narrative irony in this scene is obvious—Harry and Tyrone have, in fact, been "that bad" for a long time and by entering the "demilitarized zone" have demonstrated that they not only live for heroin, but are willing to die for it.

The scene is also crucial to the social protest level of the novel. Selby seeks to dramatize in as brutally realistic a manner as possible the potential of heroin to dehumanize those addicted to it. Even more important, he is, like Algren in *The Man with the Golden Arm,* intent on demonstrating that the drug trade flourishes in America because the capitalistic system, and those in charge of it, want and need it. The addict is made dependent on a commodity that in turn commodifies him or her—heroin is shot into the body, which becomes the literal and corrupted host for a deadly commercial product. That drugs, while ostensibly outlawed, are an officially sanctioned part of the structure of American capitalism is made manifest through the "demilitarized zone," which is sanctioned by the city government and patrolled by the police. The novel's unmistakable implication is that every city in America designates a comparable area—that in the final analysis all of America is a "demilitarized zone." Selby depicts the drug traffic as functioning through artificially induced laws of supply and demand—those in control of it create a remorseless cycle: periods of abundance in which prices are comparatively low followed by periods of scarcity in which the addict is charged exorbitant amounts for a "hit." The logic of the cycle is obvious—during the periods of abundance addicts are recruited and made

UNDERSTANDING HUBERT SELBY, JR.

to believe that what they need will always be easily obtainable; after becoming addicted, they are willing to pay whatever they are asked to feed their habit and to do whatever they must to acquire the necessary money. They thereby surrender control of their lives to the manipulators of the narcotics market and to the capitalistic system of which it is an essential part.

While *Requiem for a Dream* succeeds in exposing the corruption inherent in the drug culture, what makes the novel unforgettable is its unflinching examination of the disintegration of Harry, Tyrone, and Marion. Ultimately not only their bodies and minds, but their very souls are destroyed by their addictions. In the novel Selby seems generally unconcerned with positing a convincing source for the excessively addictive nature of their personalities. As in *The Room,* he suggests, but without a great deal of obvious conviction, a Freudian explanation for all three— it is certainly undeniable that Harry has in Sara Goldfarb a suffocating mother; Tyrone still feels the pain of losing his mother ("ol moms"), who died when he was a child; and Marion is almost stereotypical in her radical resentment of her upper-class parents. Ultimately though, all three young people exhibit, until heroin begins to erase their personalities, more sexual health than the characters in any of Selby's three earlier novels. Again, they can be more instructively approached as victims of the same factors that overwhelm virtually all of Selby's creations, a profound emptiness at the very heart of America and of "the sin of pride" that enables them to deny the existential responsibility of asserting ethical control over their lives.

While similarly guilty of pride and existential denial, Sara Goldfarb emerges as Selby's most sympathetic character largely because the external factors that contribute to her destruction are so obvious and so overwhelming. A widow with an irresponsible son, she is also savagely victimized by American capitalism. The novel opens with yet another enactment of a recurring scene—Harry and Tyrone come to Sara's apartment in order to steal her television, which they then pawn for drug money. To expedite the theft, Harry locks his mother in the closet, symbolically foreshadowing the manner in which her already narrow life will become more and more restricted until, in a very real sense, she ceases to exist at all. Harry knows but chooses not to care that he could hardly assault his mother's peace of mind in a more fundamental way. Watching television and eating chocolate have become the two defining poles of Sara's existence.

As her son knows she will be, she is quickly able to reclaim the television set, only to set in motion a chain of events more horrendous than anything Harry could ever cause her. She receives one day a phone call from "Lyle Russel of the McDick Corporation" (25), who promises her that she will soon be asked to appear as a guest on an unspecified television program. The satire in this episode is as angry as anything in *Last Exit to Brooklyn,* if less cosmic in its target of attack. Here, and indeed in all of *Requiem for a Dream,* Selby writes from a vision of America comparable to that which dominates the best work of Norman Mailer. In his fourth novel Selby is intent upon investigating the power to control and destroy individuals that is inherent in what Mailer had prophesied in *The Armies of the Night* (1968) as the possible, if not probable, advent of "the most fearsome totalitarianism the world has ever known."[7] For both writers, as well as for the postmodernist Thomas Pynchon in *The*

Crying of Lot 49, American society is in the control of a vast corporate conspiracy that masterfully and anonymously uses technology to manage its citizens. "Lyle Russel" is never more than a disembodied voice with which Sara is never again able to make contact; but in its one manifestation it masterfully induces dependency and obligation in the vulnerable woman:

> I know how you feel Mrs. Goldfarb. Believe me when I say I am just as thrilled as you to be a part of this fantastic industry. I consider myself one of the luckiest men in the world because every day I get a chance to help people just like yourself, Mrs. Goldfarb, to be a part of programming that not only are we proud of but the entire industry—no, the entire nation is proud of. . . . I know how you feel, you are wondering why you should be so lucky when so many millions would give anything to be on one of these [McDick-sponsored] shows. . . . Well, Mrs. Goldfarb, I cant tell you why you are so lucky, I guess its just that God has a special place in his heart for you. (25–26)

Selby's intended reader will be disgusted at the transparency of this technological con game, while understanding the clearly well researched effectiveness of its appeal to a lonely middle-class television addict like Sara. The phone message makes cynical use of key phrases from American popular culture and religion that are certain to resonate in Sara's highly sentimental consciousness. For instance, the words "I consider myself one of the luckiest men in the world" constitute an almost direct quotation from the famous speech of the great, terminally ill first

REQUIEM FOR A DREAM

baseman Lou Gehrig to the fans in Yankee Stadium. (Gehrig actually said, "I consider myself one of the luckiest men on the face of the earth.") Gehrig's speech became truly central to American popular culture after it was repeated by Gary Cooper, the foremost Hollywood embodiment of silent male heroism, in the 1942 film version of the baseball star's life, *The Pride of the Yankees.* Thus a masculine icon of stoic courage repeated the words of a tragic icon of selfless male bravery. After such a lead-in it is not difficult for the phone voice to set up a syllogism in which loyalty to McDick's television products equals loyalty to "the nation."

Of course, the voice belongs to the ephemeral Lyle Russel, representing an invisible corporation that certainly does not have a special place in its heart for Sara, rather than to God. Yet Selby, like the Mailer of *The Armies of the Night* and the Pynchon of *The Crying of Lot 49,* implies that such omnipresent corporations have attained godlike power in American society. Further the assertion by the phone voice that "millions would give anything to be on one of these shows" is absolutely correct. Soon the promise of future fame makes Sara a celebrity in her apartment complex. A group of other widows living there regularly sits outside in the sun while awaiting the day's mail delivery; and, upon hearing about Sara's miraculous call, they begin to live in the dim shadow of her anticipated "fame." Selby is satirizing the degree to which television has transformed America into a vicarious society, one that lives through the projected lives of its "celebrities."

The name, "McDick Corporation," is, of course, not chosen by accident—Selby is echoing the street or slang term to "dick," or to cheat and manipulate, someone. American capitalism's power to control through an increasingly ubiquitous technology is shown in *Requiem for a Dream* to be as an inescapable nightmare. Sara Goldfarb, so devoted to television that she obsessively watches the commercials, could hardly be a more perfect candidate for such control and manipulation. She, like other characters in naturalistic fiction, is ultimately victimized by a combination of external and internal forces—her obsessiveness and her vanity join with American consumerism to destroy her. Sara becomes more overtly sympathetic than other Selby characters in part because the social and cultural roots of her vanity are so clear. Now lonely and missing the male figures who once filled her life, she is the product of a paternalistic religious tradition and of a chauvinistic society that valorizes youth and beauty.

Her addiction to chocolate has distanced her from the ideal of attractiveness that is relentlessly shown her in the televised images of American consumerism. After she is unable to control her eating problem by dieting, she turns inevitably to a commercial product, diet pills, for help. As a consequence she begins to starve herself and inexorably surrenders what remains of her identity to hallucination. Selby dramatizes Sara's retreat from sanity through an especially inventive reversal of the concept of commodification—she comes to believe that her refrigerator and her television set are talking to her and are threatening to extinguish her. Moreover she is last seen in the novel as a mindless commodity trapped in an inhuman mental institution.

One of the novel's most powerful and ironic scenes occurs when Harry, at the moment when he believes that he has triumphed in the drug trade and is finally absolutely safe, comes to visit Sara after a long absence in order to tell her that he has bought a new television set for her. It does not take him long to intuit her addiction to the diet pills; and he better than most people, of course, knows what will happen to her if she does not stop using such an addictive substance. He briefly tries to convince her to give up the pills; but, after she begins to smother him as she always has with questions about a future wife and children, he finds it necessary to escape her presence. Harry can see what is happening to his mother, while being oblivious to the inevitable result of his own heroin addiction. He has an impulse to rescue Sara but quickly abandons it because her demands are so strong and unrelenting. For him, saving her would simply be too much trouble.

Moreover the television set which he brings her is simply a manifestation of the forces that have set in motion her destruction. That Harry is himself a loyal consumer of the legal as well as the illicit produces of American capitalism is evident in his near manipulation by the Macys salesman from whom he buys the new television for Sara. He refuses the salesman's urging to buy a "complete home-entertainment system with an am-fm radio," (132), but later he feels guilty about his refusal. In addition, he feels that his identity has been freshly validated by his purchase: "[he] smiled to himself as he watched himself sitting there [at the salesman's desk], taking care of himself just like a real people" (132). Thus Harry believes, like his mother and so many actual Americans, that his essential reality can only be proven through active consumerism. Ironically it is the fragile nature of his economic position that he seeks to escape through heroin.

UNDERSTANDING HUBERT SELBY, JR.

Eventually Sara can no longer stand waiting for another call from Lyle Russel and, reduced by hunger and ridiculous dress and make-up to a grotesque apparition, she invades the very sanctuary of the McDick corporation demanding that they fulfill their promise to her, that they grant her the "celebrity" identity for which she has sacrificed all else. Selby augments this scene's considerable inherent power with a compassionate lyricism: "Sara Goldfarb looked like a pitiful and soggy bag of misery and despair and she slowly sank into a chair and her tears started to mingle with the melted sleet that was dripping down her face and falling onto the bodice of her red dress, the gown she wore at Harrys bar mitzvah . . ." (214). Not knowing or caring who this pathetic figure is, the corporation turns her over to Bellevue Hospital where the final stages of her dehumanization occur.

The scenes depicting the institutional destruction of Sara are among the most powerful in the novel and complete Selby's vision of a capitalistic society that controls and destroys the individuals who reside in it. Again a reading of *Requiem for a Dream* based on the ideas central to Michel Foucault's *Discipline and Punish* would yield interesting and profitable results. The unifying motif in Selby's novel is that American capitalism rests upon certain unifying structures that are ultimately antagonistic to the welfare of its individual citizens. There is a brutal interrelationship, the novel implicitly argues, between the excesses of American consumerism as illustrated by television and advertising, the illicit drug trade, and a dehumanizing institution such as Bellevue. The police *do* supervise the distribution of heroin by the mob in the harrowing scenes depicting the end of the panic; and in Bellevue the accurate diagnosis of Sara's condition by a young doctor is overruled by a senior physician who decides that she is suffering from schizophrenia and needs electric shock treatments. The novel describes Sara's shock treatments as graphically and memorably as it does the nightmarish streets of the drug trade: "Sara could feel her bones snapping and smell the burning of her own flesh as barbed hooks were thrust into her eyes yanking them out of their sockets and all she could do was endure and feel the pain and smell the burning flesh . . ." (237). After a prolonged cycle of such treatments, Sara is reduced to a zombielike creature virtually unrecognizable to two of the widows from her complex when they visit her in Bellevue. Reading the harrowing accounts of Sara's sadistic mistreatment in the mental institution in the specific context of her established loneliness might cause a reader to view her as pure victim bearing no responsibility for her fate. Yet the essential logic of the novel requires that one remember her instant and complete participation in the McDick Corporation's seduction of her. Just as he does with Harry, Tyrone, and Marion, Selby narrates Sara's story by subtly combining detached third-person and idiomatic first-person voices.

Sara's idiomatic voice shows her to be, at the beginning of the novel, a likeable, if slightly ridiculous, woman completely devoted to the superficial values of the capitalistic society in which she lives. She takes her icons from the world of popular culture, dreaming of looking "*Zophtic*" like Rita Hayworth and of "winning" Robert Redford on the television quiz show. Her world seems void of any genuine spiritual depth. While she almost certainly adopted her husband's and her culture's values,

UNDERSTANDING HUBERT SELBY, JR.

she is still controlled by her vanity and thus represents a perfect target for manipulation by the McDick Corporation. Kenneth John Atchity offers a perceptive and concise summary of the interrelationship between Sara's values and her destruction: "So desperate is Sara for a better vision, that she has sacrificed the little good she possessed for the good at the other end of the line. When that good, like her son's heroin, proves a false good, Sara is destroyed by her own sacrifice" (404).

It is important to note Selby's dedication to *Requiem for a Dream:* "This book is dedicated, with/love, to Bobby, who has found/the only pound of pure—Faith in a Loving God." Selby's underlying vision in this novel is consistent with that contained in his other work: American society has become entrapped in the pervasive materialism of a ubiquitous capitalism, and such a world is closed to any healing or saving Grace. Thus the inhabitants of this particular "waste land" lose their souls and often their lives pursuing false and empty promises of salvation. Clearly the Selby of this novel is no longer the embittered author of *Last Exit to Brooklyn* who hated God.

Selby's resolution of the Harry and Tyrone plot is somewhat forced and contrived. Attempting to drive to Florida to get drugs, they are arrested in an unnamed southern state. Consequently, Harry dies from infection in his arm, and Tyrone is sentenced to the chain gang. Still, *Requiem for a Dream* is a generally successful novel uniquely combining naturalistic social protest with a predominantly existentialist message. Its conventional structure helps to communicate an urgent warning of the insidious addictiveness on which American consumer culture is based. Paul Metcalf to the contrary, the novel's narrative mode is not at all conventional. The innovative nature and purpose of *Requiem for a Dream*'s idiomatic narration has been analyzed most perceptively by Kenneth Tindall:

> In other kinds of books and in real life persons may be thought of as being prisoners of their context. In Selby's *Requiem for a Dream* they are prisoners of their idiom. So restricted by their language (the book reads like one of Racine's tragedies with their stripped-down vocabulary) does their possibility for conceiving ways out appear that the problem seems almost one of philology.[8]

Still, Selby dramatizes "the problem" not in the language of "philology," but in that of art. Moreover he does so with such success that the only lasting regret one feels upon finishing it is that Selby has yet to write another novel.

CHAPTER SIX

Song of the Silent Snow

Generally neglected by the critical establishment, *Song of the Silent Snow* is the great surprise of the Selby canon. While its fifteen stories cumulatively echo the major themes of the four novels and the volume's central characters are once again consumed by anger and guilt, the collection nevertheless represents in some significant ways a surprising departure from Selby's other work. For instance, the repressed violence that threatens to erupt in irrational ways—as in the four novels—is in these stories usually dissipated before any real damage occurs; and, in three stories where it does ultimately explode, the dominant narrative tone, a form of black humor, produces largely comic results. Moreover the volume is dominated by a considerably more gentle and lyrical tone than Selby had previously utilized; in fact, one especially memorable entry, "Of Whales and Dreams," is in essence a brief prose poem that in theme and language recalls the works of Walt Whitman and Thomas Wolfe. In most of the other and longer stories, this gentleness is less overt—Selby is still, after all, depicting a society so bombarded with images, if not actual experiences, of violence and mass death that it has become almost narcotized by them. The middle-class antihero of "A Little Respect" reads a paper on the subway home: "He read about a flood, a hatchet murder, an earthquake that killed 10,000 people, and relaxed."[1]

In addition to these familiar Selby motifs of latent violence and barely suppressed rage, and certainly connected with them,

various kinds and degrees of psychological trauma and alienation are evoked in the collection. Several stories depict
characters so overwhelmed by emotional anxiety and suffering, as well as by spiritual dread, that they have virtually lost
contact with any external reality. That these characters represent widely contrasting social and economic levels illustrates
the pervasive nature of such psychological and spiritual
suffering in the wasteland of twentieth-century American
society. In the volume's title story a middle-class character
struggles to recover from a near-total breakdown induced by
nervous exhaustion and at one point wonders "No one was dying,
so why cry? Or was he dying? Were there certain types of death
he knew nothing about?" (205) Like Selby's four novels *Song of
the Silent Snow* is an exploration of the various kinds of death, and
death-in-life, plaguing modern American society.

Yet the third-person narrative voice here is more openly
compassionate toward, and forgiving of, Selby's lost and tormented characters than the one recounting the brutality and
suffering in the four novels. More than once in the fifteen stories,
it encourages identification with their pain. Selby's hatred of God
that so dominates and even shapes *Last Exit to Brooklyn* and *The
Room* has been largely displaced by the emphasis upon love that
first began to emerge in *Requiem for a Dream*. This significant
variation on Selby's aesthetic does nothing to modify his vision
of the urban twentieth-century as a severely restricted world; in
fact, one finds in *Song of the Silent Song* a more complex kind of
determinism than that which dominates his novels. In these
stories an overwhelming and crushing environmental determinism often yields to explorations of psychological suffering.

The origins of the characters' psychological alienation, usually moments of intense and individual early suffering, are as varied as the individual characters themselves. Selby's narrator sometimes, but certainly not always, offers overt hints about the specific nature of these individual traumas. When such damaged characters encounter economic oppression as in "The Coat," the volume's longest story and one of its best, no hope can exist for their ultimate recovery. Yet, as has been noted, for the first time in Selby's work several of the stories evoke a sense of affirmation and hope. Bill Langenheim, in a 1988 interview with Selby, states, "It wasn't until I read the stories in *Song* that I began to see the introduction of hope in your characters' lives."[2] He adds that this new mode of affirmation is especially evident in the short, lyrical "Of Whales and Dreams":

> In the story you talk about a kid who wants to see the whales, to ship out and see first hand the whales. It was his personal dream as a boy. And he does. He gets his. The story is about salvation through one's dreams, and about the beauty of their life-affirming hope. (27–28)

Selby does not disagree with Langenheim's analysis. While satire is as central to this volume as it is to the novels, it is for the most part a new, at least for Selby, mode of satire, which in one story explodes in a unique combination of vaudevillian slapstick and absurdist black humor. While there are certainly overtly comic moments in Selby's four novels (for example, the brief "And Baby Makes Three" segment of *Last Exit to Brooklyn* as well as parts of that novel's coda, "Landsend"), the endings of a few of the stories in *Song of the Silent Snow* represent a distinct and innovative departure in his work, constituting moments of unexpected comic release for the reader.

One should not, of course, be surprised to discover Selby's talent for writing short fiction, since several of the segments that comprise *Last Exit to Brooklyn* were initially published in "little magazines."[3] What makes *The Song of the Silent Snow* uniquely rewarding is its incorporation of several levels of fictional tone and social setting. The volume takes on the unique coherence of rich diversity. For instance, several major male characters with socio-economic backgrounds ranging from homelessness to the upper middle class are named (what else?) Harry. Whether living on the streets or in the suburbs, they all, with one significant exception, are brought to a debilitating confrontation with their fundamental powerlessness and impotence. Collectively, they, like Harry Black in *Last Exit to Brooklyn,* Harry White in *The Demon,* and Harry Goldfarb in *Requiem for a Dream,* embody Selby's weak and vulnerable urban male.

Langenheim's interview with Selby contains a revealing, if somewhat tongue-in-cheek, exchange. After the novelist has mentioned Dante, Langenheim shares an insight with his subject, ". . . you've been taking this guy Harry and hammering him into the ground now for almost twenty-five years." The interviewer then asks, "are you ever going to take Harry out of the Inferno and put him in Paradise?" Selby's answer is amused and noncommittal: "I may, what the hell. [Laughs] I guess that's the least I can do for Harry. Yeah, that would be nice" (28). Selby cannot, of course, remove "Harry" from the urban hell of America and still be true to his art; the inferno in which his people are trapped is every bit as eternal and inescapable as is the one created by Dante. In fact, the individuals who inhabit the hells depicted by both writers share some of the same sins.

In addition to the structural coherence that the recurrent character of "Harry" gives it, the volume achieves further unity through certain subtle structural devices. It opens with a brief, savage incident of childhood entitled "Fat Phils Day," in which Selby employs a game of craps played by boys as a metaphor for the story's narrative strategy in the same way he does the game of mum in *Last Exit to Brooklyn*. In fact, the boys in "Fat Phils Day" seem younger versions of the members of *Last Exit to Brooklyn*'s violent, raging street gang. As depicted in this brief episode, childhood in the sketch is clearly Darwinian, a struggle in which the physically weak survive and even triumph through sheer cunning. Beyond an animalistic formula for survival, the story offers nothing hopeful or affirmative. Its world is defined by a kind of primitive and unforgiving capitalism, as exemplified in the game of craps.

In sharp contrast is the penultimate piece in the collection, also a brief sketch, "Of Whales and Dreams." While not literally about childhood, it is certainly related to that favorite subject of poets and writers. Unashamedly lyrical, "Of Whales and Dreams" is rooted in the the nineteenth-century American transcendentalism of Emerson, Thoreau, and Whitman—it affirms and celebrates the presence of a mystical unity between human beings and nature, and indeed flowing throughout the universe. The narrator begins the sketch by recalling the childhood moment when he was warned that to "deny [his] dream" would be "to sell [his] soul" (195). Remembering this advice, "in his mid-teens" he "finally went to sea" (196).

The remainder of the sketch consists primarily of Selby's elaboration of an extended metaphor that in its audacity and "serious" playfulness recalls the "conceits" so central to the art of the seventeenth-century British metaphysical poets. Reminiscing about watching whales explode to the surface of the sea, the narrator indulges himself in a fantasy: "in my head I would be playing a song on a concertina and pipe, teaching them to dance, and they honked their glee as they whirled and twirled through the water waving their flukes in time and merriment to the music. . . ." In a transcendental sense this might in fact not be a fantasy at all; a moment of spiritual bonding with nature as described by Emerson or Whitman might well result in the literally and divinely inspired writer directing the creatures of nature in play.

Selby completes his metaphor by asserting, again like Emerson and Whitman (not to mention literary critics down to and including Harold Bloom), that such divine play is the ultimate human answer to death: "and they wave their flukes at me and we dance and laugh and this thing called death no longer exists, being dissolved in our oneness . . . and my life is theirs and theirs mine, and we are all part of the same dream" (197). An obvious assumption is that Selby's transcendent play here is his art, as harsh and uncompromisingly naturalistic as it often is. In it, Selby is free to imagine, if only for brief, fleeting moments, that "life" is "large and strong and beautiful and full of gentleness and joy." Of course, the body of his fiction, including most of the stories in *Song of the Silent Snow,* emphasizes the ways in which the grim reality of modern urban existence commonly perverts such "gentleness and joy."

UNDERSTANDING HUBERT SELBY, JR.

While human beings are potentially redeemed by a universal love, in Selby's world, the sheer brutality of existence generally obscures, if not completely destroys, any real or lasting awareness of the salvation to be found in such love, generally leaving his people with only an inchoate and consequently maddening sense of a tantalizing, unknowable redemption. Manifesting itself in diverse forms, a pervasive psychological and spiritual alienation is the inevitable result of the relentless frustration of "the same dream" in which we all share. The central unifying motif of *Song of the Silent Snow* is an exploration of the diverse forms that such alienation can take. The volume explores, sometimes in a quite clinical manner, manifestations of mental illness ranging from chronic long-term depression, or dysthymia, to profound schizophrenia. For the first time in all of Selby's work, the concluding title story of the volume describes a process of healing and escape from alienation and pain.

In "Song of the Silent Snow," the central character, inevitably named Harry, is an apparently quite successful businessman who, before the story opens, suffered a profound psychological breakdown which has been diagnosed by his doctor as a form of "nervous exhaustion" (204). His collapse was triggered by the purchase of an expensive house in the suburbs of Connecticut, an act which caused unbearable stress and a debilitating insomnia. When the story opens, his insomnia has been alleviated by drugs, but he remains debilitated, unable to work and terrified of any expression of closeness or affection from his wife and two sons.

He has started to realize though that the purchase of the house was only one symptom of a much deeper and more totalizing fear: "He was suddenly so overwhelmed by the responsibility of love . . . the responsibility of living" (204). Essentially Harry is, in fact, a familiar, if no longer necessarily sympathetic, figure—the male head of a nuclear family who is exhausted by the relentless pressures of a capitalistic social structure, especially the demands of his job and the expectations that he will provide security and comfort for his family. He is a prototype of the middle-class male who has never had the time or the wherewithall simply to get tired and rest for a while. Despite his new awareness, he still struggles to place his suffering in a rational context: "No one was dying, so why cry? Or was he dying? Were there certain types of death he knew nothing about? Was it possible to stay like this forever" (205)?

Of course, he *is* dying spiritually, in a much quieter and more passive way than Selby's people usually do, but dying nevertheless. In the story's climax Harry, performing the only kind of sustained physical activity of which he is now capable, is walking through a gentle snowfall when the "song" of the falling snow, which "he knew very few had ever heard" (213), encourages him to simply surrender and escape all his pain at once: "he knew he could stay here forever" (213).

Gradually, though, he becomes aware of "another sound, vague at first but then more and more familiar as he heard it within him" (213). This second sound, significantly coming from within him rather than from any external source, heralds his healing and salvation; it is the song that arises out of the happiness of life with his family. It has slowly been forcing its way to the surface of his consciousness for some time. In the story's conclusion he embraces it and rushes home to his wife and children. While more subtle and considerably less lyrical than "Of Whales and Dreams,"

UNDERSTANDING HUBERT SELBY, JR.

"Song of the Silent Snow" holds out hope and affirmation to the reader. The world depicted here, parallel in strict social terms to the one so harshly evoked in *The Demon,* is finally a forgiving one. It is certainly far different than the Darwinian environment seen in "Fat Phils Day."

Nervous exhaustion is only one of the clinical states that Selby describes in *Song of the Silent Snow;* and none of the other victims attains the kind of psychic healing that Harry so unexpectedly discovers among the gently falling snow. Still, in the second half of the volume, Selby's compassion for his characters becomes increasingly overt (certainly more so than in the novels); and he begins to grant his people a kind of ironic peace, which allows them to endure at least the loneliness and pain of existence.

In contrast the stories in the first half of the volume recall the more familiar Selby mode of unrelenting despair. "Fat Phils Day" is immediately followed by "Hi Champ," which chronicles the way in which a single and lonely man, Harry Lewis, allows his depression and sexual insecurity to destroy his relationship with an attractive woman who seems genuinely to like him. Unable to believe that Rita might be impressed with him simply for who he is, he takes her to Jack Dempsey's restaurant, having gone to great trouble beforehand to arrange for Dempsey, the former heavyweight champion, to stop at their table and speak to him by name. After Dempsey leaves, Harry tries to create the impression that he is a friend of the boxer's, although Dempsey routinely does the same thing for any customer who asks. Selby is a master at catching the kind of ridiculous and painfully trite dialogue that inevitably arises in this kind of situation:

SONG OF THE SILENT SNOW

Rita smiled, I didnt know you knew Jack Dempsey.
Well, we/re not exactly bosom buddies, but . . . you know.
I think thats terrific. Im really impressed.
Harry smiled and nodded in acceptance of the compliment.
Hes really a very nice guy you know. I mean a regular guy.
I like the way he speaks. I guess I must have been expect-
ing some sort of rough—she shrugged her shoulders—
certainly not such a nice, gentle man.
Yeah, the movies have tended to stereotype certain—.
(19–20)

In a subsequent bit of dialogue, Rita, while discussing
the classic horror movie *The Bride of Frankenstein,* unknow-
ingly anticipates the story's ending: "[Frankenstein] didnt
want much, did he? Just someone to share what he had with.
Funny how simple it seems sometimes to be happy and yet
how easily it all gets confused" (22). For someone like Harry
Lewis, it gets extremely confused very quickly. After spend-
ing the night with Rita, he is the next morning for a brief time
intensely happy and promises to call her later. Then the
narration takes the reader inside Harry's mind to observe the
gradual way in which his depression and insecurity inexorably destroy any possibility of a genuine and lasting relationship with Rita. His thought process begins with this joyous
but telling exclamation: "It almost seemed unreal. God what a
night . . . What a woman . . . What a joy" (25).

He then proceeds to convince himself that "it" is indeed
"unreal." He begins by assuring himself that Rita could only have
been impressed with him because she believed that he was a

friend of Dempsey's. Next he decides that she has caught his lie about knowing Dempsey and is in the process of dumping him in disgust. Actually there is no real evidence in the story that Rita particularly admires the fighter. Still Harry sums up the entire evening to himself as a "lie" and concludes that "Theres no point in calling. Its always the same . . . its all over" (26). For a man like Harry Lewis, it will, in fact, always be the same, or it will be until he gets some meaningful help for his depression and insecurity. Selby is *at least* as good as any other contemporary American writer in delineating the pathology of this kind of lonely, self-defeating middle-class urban male.

In contrast "Fortune Cookie," a study of the capacity for obsession in a struggling salesman, ends on an ironically positive note. The Harry of this story shares a comparable social and economic background with Harry of "Song of the Silent Snow" and is saved from the same kind of mental and spiritual collapse only by his seemingly infinite capacity for self-deception. He is denied though anything close to the peace that descends, along with the falling snow, on the Harry of the volume's concluding story. As the story opens he is seated "in a rear booth of [a] . . . Chinese restaurant, alone and worried" and arriving at something that "was more than an anxiety" (41). He is confronting an unavoidable fact: "A salesman sells. It is that simple. A salesman sells and when he doesnt he is not a salesman and who needs a salesman who is not selling" (41). The theme and even the language of Arthur Miller's *Death of a Salesman* echoes in these lines; and in "Fortune Cookie" Selby joins Miller and the David Mamet of *Glengarry Glen Ross* in creating definitive images of the kind of calculated and relentless insecurity that haunts the life of a salesman.

SONG OF THE SILENT SNOW

Things briefly change for Selby's protagonist after he opens his fortune cookie and reads, "Take courage, today is your day for success" (42). He decides that indeed "It has to be somebodys day and Ive had enough losers" (42). Quickly two things happen: Harry makes a big sale and immediately becomes addicted to fortune cookies. Soon though, the fortune cookie messages start becoming ambiguous and even a little ominous, and Harry quickly loses his newfound confidence. The little slips of paper constitute for the salesman Harry the same kind of trap that Jack Dempsey's name does for Harry Lewis—each character desperately adopts a sign or talisman of success that momentarily reassures him but also enables him to deny that the real source of his success is internal, to deny in effect his inherent worth. To complicate things further, Harry also develops "Chinese restaurant syndrome"—he becomes nauseated as a result of eating nothing but Chinese food.

In desperation, he briefly talks himself out of desiring success at the executive level; but, fittingly by sheer chance, he is delivered from his own misgivings when he discovers an affirmative horoscope in the daily newspaper. While the dominant mode of "Fortune Cookie" is obviously more comic than that of "Hi Champ"; the central figures in both stories share the same essential problem, each is dependent upon external and quite arbitrary signifiers of self-worth. Neither is ready to accept the challenge of constructing a strong identity.

"Liebesnacht" (Love Night) is a more complex story recalling in its characterization and climactic explosion into violence the Selby of *Last Exit to Brooklyn*. It opens with its "Harry" engaging in and even helping to provoke a telephone fight with his girlfriend, of course named Mary, so that instead of having to take her out he can go drinking with his male buddies. As far as sexual enlightenment and basic tolerance go, this Harry is a typical Selby male; after the argument is finished and Mary has hung up, he mutters "you crazy bitch, you . . . you . . . ah, who needsya" (68) into his now safely silent receiver. At STEVES, a neighborhood bar, the young men participate in some revealing mock homosexual banter: "Yeah, well its early yet. The night is young." "And youre so beautiful. Kelly pinched Larrys cheek and they chuckled and reached for their beers" (971).

Together in an exclusively male conclave, the gang can deny any potentially genuine and thus disturbing feelings by mocking them in advance. Moreover it would not be at all surprising to learn that, like the street gang of *Last Exit to Brooklyn,* they sometimes engage in certain homosexual acts while loudly proclaiming their heterosexuality. At any rate, their conversation concerning women is a frightening mixture of bravado and latent violence:

[A young man named Kelly]: One thing you cant do is let a broad break ya balls . . . Ya gotta keepem in their place or they/ll shove it in and break it off.
[Harry]: Yeah, yeah, I know man . . . gettin laid aint worth all that bullshit.
[Kelly]: Ya goddamn right. Ya gotta letem know whos the fuckin boss. . . .
[Harry:] Hey, right on man. Take it from me, ya either slapem down or cutem loose. (75)

Selby has perfected this kind of brutal and absurd drunken male dialogue.

It is somewhat surprising then that Harry does not turn out to be the center of violence in the story. That role is instead taken by a remarkable figure known in the neighborhood as "Mikey no legs":

> Although he was called no legs, it was not an accurate description. It was simply that he had a large barrel chest . . . and his legs appeared too short for his body.
>
> He wasn't exceptionally violent or quiet, jut sort of unobtrusively there, except when he got crazy drunk. Fortunately he only got drunk periodically, and then it was only occasionally that he got violent, when some twisted message tripped through his drunken body to his brain and voices burned his head and he couldnt scream them quiet, and, from time to time, things would appear without or within his head that he had to defend himself against. (71–72)

In his creation of Mikey, Selby seems to echo Steinbeck's Lennie of *Of Mice and Men,* an inherently gentle man except when his mental deficiency abruptly asserts itself. Also in both characterizations, external grotesqueness is emblematic of internal deformity and danger.

Unable to get or hold any job outside the house, Mikey has spent his life helping his older brother Wally, whom he almost worships, carry outside the huge garbage cans from his family's apartment building. Wally fully shares in this fraternal devotion and spends much of his time trying to protect others from Mikey and Mikey from himself. He is not always successful in this endeavor though, and before the story opens his brother has in a drunken rage badly injured Wally's hand. At the bar with the others, Wally can forget the pain in his hand and be relieved at the certainty that Mikey, after he sobers up, will not remember anything about the incident. Wally's relief turns out to be short-lived though; abruptly Mikey appears in the bar and demands to know who hurt his brother's hand, and Wally understands that he is trapped in a dilemma that is virtually guaranteed to end violently: "If he told [Mikey] somebody did it to him he would want to know who, and if Wally didnt give him a name sooner or later Mike would decide that somebody walking the street did it and might try and kill him" (77–78).

Mikey no legs functions in the story as a personification of the id of the young men who inhabit the bar and of Harry in particular. When drunk, he commits the kind of irrational violence that Harry and the others are generally content simply to threaten. Moreover his bond of loyalty to Wally replicates in miniature the unspoken code of loyalty Wally shares with his friends. The grotesque nature of his physical appearance images the grotesque and sordid nature of the values of the young men who inhabit STEVES. The nickname "no legs" echoes the incompleteness and inadequacy of these values.

Ultimately Wally can think of nothing to do except tell Mikey the truth, and, of course, the younger brother is instantly stricken with a degree of guilt verging on insanity. As the group of young men walk down the street after leaving the bar, they encounter a young man and woman, clearly lovers. Seeing a way to make things up to his brother; he grabs a splintered piece of two-by-four and rushes the terrified couple, telling the young man to leave and proclaiming to the young woman that he and his brother are going to rape her. After Wally and the others step him in and barely succeed in saving the situation, he is simply baffled: "I mean, what the fuck Wally, it/ll take ya mind off ya hand, right" (83). Mikey no legs lacks sufficient linguistic sophistication to understand that the verbal violence of Wally and his companions is empty and displaced. Frustrated in his attempt to obtain sexual gratification for his brother, he explodes into rage and attacks a newsstand, screaming primally as he does so. Mikey's scream is delivered for all the story's adolescent "men," who avoid confronting their emotional inadequacy and their resulting fear of sexual failure.

It clearly constitutes a release of tension for Harry, who retreats to the river at Sixty-ninth Street, searching for the now-vanished pier of his childhood. There, much like the older Harry of "Hi Champ," he reassures himself that Mary is undoubtedly at that moment having sex with someone else and surrenders to his loneliness. The story's protagonist ends by embracing an illusion of perpetual childhood in which he will be able to avoid complexity. The fundamental immaturity and temporariness of his life is foreshadowed when he finds satisfaction by urinating and "carving" a "near perfect (to him) H" in a cake of ice at the bottom of the urinal (73). Harry's life is essentially an exercise in egotism, a waste. The only genuine passion in his "love night" is self-love. Again, Selby's unique genius is his ability to depict this familiar type of urban young man with understanding and compassion. "Liebesnacht" is one of the best stories in the volume, a rich exercise of craft and vision.

It is immediately followed by another beautifully sustained investigation into the ramifications of pain and alienation, "The Sound." In his 1992 interview with Allan Vorda, Selby mentions something that would not have been at all hard to guess—"The Sound" is "where the concept for . . . [*The Room*] started" and then describes its structure as "variations on a musical theme."[4]

Like *The Room,* "The Sound" opens with its focal and essentially only character, whose last name the reader will eventually learn is Mr. Rawls, in jail. He awakens, like the protagonist of Selby's second novel, locked in a "9 by 6 room." He is confused and terrified, trying desperately to understand what shocked him out of his sleep. "Something awakened him, but what? A dream? He tried remembering. . . . Nothing. It couldn't have been a dream . . ." (89). The remainder of the story recounts Rawls's struggle to understand the nature of the terror that tortures his subconscious and two related matters, where he is and how long he has been there. Such an experience is hardly new for him: "He had awakened so many times in unfamiliar places with no memory of how he had gotten there . . ." (102). He rather quickly gets a frightening clue concerning the first mystery: "The sound must be real. It couldn't be his imagination" (90). Briefly he is calmed by the realization that he is in a locked room, believing that the source of the noise will not be able to reach him.

Returning to the comfort of sleep, Rawls dreams of "almost forgotten . . . ancient memories" (94), specifically one of fishing with his father. His images of that time are pastoral, even bucolic, evoking Mark Twain's *Tom Sawyer* and Ernest Hemingway's Nick Adams stories. He is next awakened by a woman informing

SONG OF THE SILENT SNOW

him that it is time for his medication. After noticing a brown envelope in the pocket of his pajamas with the words "COUNTY JAIL" printed on it, he gradually remembers that he has been in the county jail hospital and deduces that he must have been arrested the night before. A familiarity with the process of being arrested and jailed is implicit in this process of deduction.

Now relieved, Rawls, with the help of the medication, is able to return mentally to the pastoral fishing scene with his father. This time, though, the reassuring memory is abruptly shattered by an ominous sound and by an image of his father disappearing into a mist. Without comprehending it, the protagonist is getting close to a shattering two-part realization. In fact, the first part becomes clear almost immediately—the sound is a prolonged scream of terror coming from inside himself. He finds himself standing by the door of his cell when this becomes clear to him, even though he has no memory of how he got there. Metaphorically he is at the door of a horrendous memory.

The story next takes a grotesque twist worthy of Edgar Allan Poe (as discussed, Selby not infrequently echoes Poe). Rawls becomes aware that he is tormented by a mysterious itching sensation and, believing that he is being assaulted by lice, convulsively tears at his flesh, leaving bloody marks over much of his body. The reader quickly comprehends that the blood is the result of deep and prolonged scratching by Rawls and that the itching moreover is an external manifestation of something even more frightening. Soon the mist reappears, and a figure starts to emerge out of it, "The features weren't distinct, but he [Rawls] was aware of a full thick beard and felt accusation burning into him" (103).

As the previously veiled image emerges more clearly, Rawls remembers that on the fishing trip, when it began to rain, he had retreated with his father to stand beneath some trees until the adult male urged him to run away. He obeyed but stopped at one point to turn around and look and then he saw the flash of lightning, "a huge oak splitting and groaning to the ground, [and] his father disappearing in the fiery flash and smoke" (104). This memory is too painful, and Rawls attempts to retreat to his childhood memories of popular culture—he imagines a Mickey Mouse–Donald Duck cartoon which is not really a cartoon and which climaxes with Mickey driving a motorcycle under the bed in pursuit of the bugs. But this escape is doomed, and Rawls soon surrenders his fragile hold on sanity.

Even if the death-by-lightning device seems somewhat forced, "The Sound" is in its totality a beautifully crafted work of short fiction. Rawls's gradual movement toward comprehension of the reality of his position and his shocking final flight from it are powerfully evoked; and Selby's creation of the initially mysterious sound as metaphor for the protagonist's childhood memories is effectively sustained. The story unforgettably explores the kind of guilt arising from traumatic childhood experience that can result in the profound psychological crippling of an adult. In his subconscious mind Rawls's childhood obedience of his father's urging him to run away seems a betrayal that caused his father's death. For him heroin provides escape from pain and guilt, but it is an escape that carries its own trap. Perhaps the strongest of several strong ingredients in "The Sound" is the compassion for victims of comparable forms of mental anguish that is implicit in every line of the story.

The next story, "I'm Being Good," which concludes the largely pessimistic first half of the volume, is another study of the debilitating effects of repressed guilt. Narrated in an epistolary manner, it describes the suffering of a woman in a mental institution. She writes regularly to her apparently unfeeling and neglectful husband, Harold; asking him in her first letter for reassurance that "the sun will come up" (109). Variations on the refrain "Im being good" dominate her letters. She even concludes her account of an unprovoked attack by another female inmate against a third woman in this way: "it was really terrible and I was scared to death but I was good" (113). Later, informed that the woman who initiated the struggle has been put "in a dungeon way way down under the building" (114), she thinks that such a medieval form of punishment might be real. One again recalls Michel Foucault here and especially his analysis of the asylum and the prison as institutions for the punishment of the soul.

When recalling the pleasures of ice cream during her childhood, the woman writes: "there was always an ice cream truck of some kind, usually a good humor. . . . I was a good girl, I really was. I was quiet" (117). The phrase "good humor" evokes a vanished age of innocence, and her equating "being good" with being "quiet" conveys much about the extreme repression that has obviously characterized her life.

The references in her letters to "being good" constitute a coded plea to Harold to rescue her from her entrapment. Approximately halfway through the story, one gets an important clue concerning the specific problem she has with her husband as well as the nature of her guilt: "I know its hard with kids yelling and screaming and running around. Maybe in a bigger place they wont upset you" (115). Finally, after futilely waiting for answers to her letters from Harold, she expresses the repressed anger which has frightened her for so long:

> O I wish you could come see me or write or something now instead of worrying about those little monsters whore always interfering in everything. . . . in the writing class [given for the inmates at the hospital] when I started to read my peace I only got to read about a page when one of the men started yelling and screaming at me that I had no right to write such silliness when children all over the world were starving and dying like flies and all kinds of horrible things he said to me and accused me as if I were some sort of monster . . . I love my children honest honest true. . . ." (119)

The protagonist is a classic victim of socially enforced gender roles—she tried to be a good little girl and keep quiet, and she has tried to be "the good mother," even though the role never fit her and in fact frustrated her creativity. She is reminiscent of central characters in American women's fiction from Kate Chopin and Charlotte Perkins Gilman to Alice Walker and Sue Miller; her imagination and her very freedom have been denied, resulting in a guilt and a repressed anger that have damaged her spiritually and psychologically. On first thought "Im Being Good," an overtly feminist work, seems a surprising story for Selby to have written. Yet when one remembers that his compassion for social victims is broadly inclusive, it seems a natural, and even an inevitable, addition to his canon.

The "slips" in the woman's writing are, in fact, not accidental; the use of "whore" rather than "who're" communicates that she has condemning herself as a "bad woman" for disobeying society's rules. Moreover, she did try to read her "peace" as well as her piece; that is, she sought to utilize the writing class as a place to find peace at last. Selby successfully utilizes her slips in language and syntax to reveal the chaotic and disordered nature of the protagonist's thought process. Her last letter communicates a descent into a total and complete irrationality.

She finally achieves "peace and quiet," but only by retreating completely into silence. Now even her childhood Christmas memories have taken on a threatening shape. The entirely passive role of Harold in this story is revealing; almost certainly his lack of responsiveness to his wife's pain and suffering contributed significantly to her destruction.

As powerful as "Liebesnacht," "The Sound," and "Im Being Good" are, perhaps the volume's richest and most eloquent study of despair is "The Coat," a painfully detailed account of a homeless man's unceasing struggle to retain possession of a battered old Salvation Army overcoat that has become "his friend, his buddy . . . his only companion" (155). The protagonist, forty-year-old Harry Wright, is in every way "wrong" for the society in which he is trapped. He has since childhood "had a difficult time being with people," largely because he is terrified of them (156). His experience as a homeless person has taught him two important lessons: that "Winter always returned" (155) and that "You had to be careful on skid row. You had to be your own council . . . your own friend:" "He didnt know how many

men he had seen beaten, and killed, for a coat or a bottle of wine"
(157). In order to bear such horror, Harry has surrendered to
alcoholism.

The plot of "The Coat" is structured around two related
motifs: the significance to Harry of an old and battered
Salvation Army coat and the various threats, legal and otherwise, to take it from him. The nature and degree of his
dependence upon the coat is emphasized early in the story
when, while drinking, he looks up from his corner in an alley
to see a rat staring at him; after driving it away, he assures
himself that the coat will prevent the rodent from attacking
him. Both literally and metaphorically cornered, he envisions
his coat as a protecting shield of armor. Harry's world is, if
possible, even more relentlessly Darwinian than Fat Phil's.
Before the story opens, he had been frightened into abandoning his "apartment," a huge wooden packing crate, by the
sounds of a fight and possible murder in the alley into which
he has carried it. After watching a scarred and battered cat
corner and kill another or perhaps the same rat, Harry takes
a drink and briefly wonders about the violence of nature
before pushing such thoughts away with still another drink.

How much Harry, a fundamentally kind and decent man,
is not meant for such a brutal universe is revealed in a scene
in which he risks his coat in attempting to save an old wino.
A gang of roving teenagers pour lighter fluid over the help-
less man and then toss a lighted match on him and run away
laughing as the bum explodes in flames. Without thinking,
Harry reacts by wrapping his coat around the suffering man.
Later the police inform the protagonist that he has, if only

temporarily, saved the bum's life. Whether the wino in fact lives or dies, Harry has established himself as one whose instinct is to preserve, rather than to destroy, human lives. His characterization is then a variation upon the type of the ironic Christ figure common in modern, and especially existential, literature. The account of his wrapping the coat around the burning man echoes the biblical description of Christ "wrapped in swaddling clothes" in the manger. After the rescue Harry retreats to the alley to comfort his damaged, though still intact, friend. "His relief was so great that he spent many, many minutes hugging and kissing his coat, telling it he was sorry if it got hurt but he had to do it, he couldnt just let the guy burn, and his coat reassured him that it was alright . . ." (166). Soon he will be forced into an even more direct understanding of how fragile his life, and indeed all life, is. Thoughtlessly walking down a street, he passes a doorway out of which two bums suddenly appear and grab him, trying to rip off his coat. He succeeds in protecting his friend but only at the cost of being kicked and beaten until he loses consciousness. At the hospital where he is taken by police, the doctors initially see no hope for him, and his heart does, in fact, momentarily stop beating. But he is revived by "an alert nurse" even though there is "no known medical explanation for his still being alive" (168). Harry's miraculous "resurrection" emphasizes his role as ironic Christ figure. It further communicates the power of his latent will to live. Thus his characterization is again linked to life and salvation. Upon regaining consciousness at Bellevue, he reveals, in an interview with the attending nurse, a surprising capacity for irony:

[Nurse:] Address?
[Harry:] The Bowery.
[Nurse:] The Bowery? Dont you have a permanent mailing address?
[Harry:] The Bowerys permanent. It aint movin. . . .
[Nurse:] In case of emergency who do you want notified?
[Harry:] I dont really care. . . . Gallo Brothers. (169)

This exchange represents a rare attempt by Harry to reach out to another human being, an urge that is squelched when he is unable to discover from an overburdened and uncaring hospital staff what happened to his coat. His questions about his "friend" become so relentless and desperate that a psychiatrist is brought in to give him an examination, which quickly becomes a hostile interrogation. Such hostility is inexplicable and frightening to Harry, who not surprisingly retreats into silence.

He spends three months in Bellevue, ostensibly being "treated," but in reality generally being ignored and allowed to sink deeper into despair. Selby is of course continuing the satiric attack against the oppressive nature of anonymous psychiatric institutions that he began in *The Room* and repeated in *Requiem for a Dream.* Such institutions do not, his fiction asserts, seek to cure but rather to repress and control. Entrapment in Bellevue shuts Harry off from the only forms of relief he knows: "[on the Bowery] the ugliness was real and the wine painted over that and he could go his way, alone, washing dishes, junking, finding some place to nest alone and talk and sing softly to himself and his coat, and drink himself to a state of unconsciousness" (175–76).

SONG OF THE SILENT SNOW

An additional level of irony in the story is the unarguable fact that Harry's view of his world and, by extension, much of American society is more accurate that the psychiatrist's. Life throughout much of America truly is, Selby seems to be saying, harsh and cruel; and Harry has in his own way simply adjusted to that reality. While the hospital does not destroy him as it does Sara Goldfarb in *Requiem for a Dream,* it does not help him either. In an exit interview Harry frustrates and angers the psychiatrist by refusing to say that he wishes to better himself. Harry briefly considers trying to explain that "he had found the most comfortable life he had ever had and was going to stay there," but instead he quietly comforts himself with the knowledge that the psychiatrist is "no longer a problem" for him (177).

His problems with Bellevue are not over, however; when he goes to pick up his clothes, they have been lost. He, of course, only cares about finding the ragged and burned coat. He nearly collapses in grief over its loss, begging for admission into the storage room in order to find the coat himself (178). Having been forced at last to notice Harry, the storage room staff looks seriously for his clothes and rather quickly finds them. At last escaping the hospital, the homeless man is wrapped securely inside his best friend and can look forward to returning to his old familiar life:

He walked carefully down the street to the first liquor store and bought a pint of muscatel. As soon as he got outside he took a drink, standing still long enough to experience it going down and through his body, knowing soon the drabness and ugliness would be tolerable. He put the bottle in his pocket and started walking toward the bus stop. Soon he would be back on the Bowery and he would find a nice deserted building to nest in and leisurely drink his wine, then softly talk and sing to himself and his coat. (179)

This concluding affirmation is extremely limited in nature. In the eyes of society Harry never has been, and never will be, "right." Yet his muted victory is simply that he knows and accepts this. He is unable and unwilling to pay the inevitable psychic costs of "bettering" himself. He does not want to be "better" than he is; he just wants to be left alone. Sadly the Darwinian world in which he is trapped will probably not let him alone for long. That he will not live much longer is a likely guess. For the moment, though, he is content; and, unlike the woman in "Im Being Good," he still retains a fragile grip on sanity. Most important, Harry Wright seems the most innocent of all Selby's suffering characters—it is difficult to see that he is in any serious way guilty of the sin of pride. He is instead clearly a victim of his environment and his psychological makeup. In this beautifully sustained piece of writing Selby risks letting his compassion show.

Other stories in *Song of the Silent Snow* are worth more extensive discussion than is possible here. "Puberty" is a sustained lyrical study of the end of childhood; in tone and language it, like "Of Whales and Dreams," recalls the work of Thomas Wolfe. In fact, it functions in the volume as a kind of transitional work between "Of Whales and Dreams" and the introductory "Fat Phils Day." "The Musician," which follows "The Coat" in the volume, is a sensitive and understated story of the frustrations and single triumph of the deferred life. In its quiet mood it echoes not Wolfe, but rather astonishingly for Selby, Henry James. "The Musician" depicts the world of fifty-three-year-old Harold, who chose not to try for a career as a concert pianist but to settle for a boring and spiritually unfulfilling desk job in order to support his two unmarried older sisters. Harold has also largely sublimated his sexuality, at least enough to channel it into relatively harmless acts such as exploring the lingerie section of his favorite department store.

At the end of the story the reader discovers that Harold's abandoning a career as a concert pianist did not constitute a major loss. Each Monday night he performs at the piano for his sisters, who are always exhilarated by his performance; however, he is fully aware that his playing lacks "the brilliance of imagination, that rush of genius that made for greatness" (191). In this story Selby explores the Jamesian theme of the centrality of the imagination in the creation of art. As in "The Coat," he provides a muted note of affirmation to relieve his central character's pain; despite his awareness of his musical limitations, Harold loves the Monday nights with his sisters. Thus the story emphasizes that, even for the artist lacking in imagination and genius, any audience, however small, makes possible the healing act of creation.

"Double Feature," "Indian Summer, and "A Little Respect" are closer to the kind of fiction one normally expects from Selby. All climax in sudden outbursts of violence, "Indian Summer" and "A Little Respect" even risking the theme of potential violence to children. Yet all three stories are finally more absurd than anything; the worst form of assault against a child occurs in

"Indian Summer" when a guilty and selfish father smacks mashed potatoes and gravy on his little girl's head. One needs only to imagine how the stupid and insensitive father will instantly feel after realizing what he has done. "A Little Respect" is black humor at its most outrageous; it ranks with the best short fiction of Bruce Jay Friedman, Terry Southern and other 1950s and 1960s specialists in this unique genre.

Song of the Silent Snow represents an interesting departure in Selby's fiction toward a more overt compassion and affirmation than is seen in the three novels. In scope, it treats virtually all socio-economic levels of urban society. An often muted but never absent affirmation underlying *Song of the Silent Snow* is expressly stated by the narrator of "Of Whales and Dreams": "we are all part of the same dream." In the collection Selby examines some of the most frequent ways in which this collective dream is frustrated and even destroyed, but he also celebrates the irrational human determination to pursue it. *Song of the Silent Snow* is a major, if little known, work of art, on an aesthetic level with anything else in Selby's canon, including *Last Exit to Brooklyn*. It moreover represents a final evolution in his art away from the European aesthetic of *The Room* toward an unmistakably American vision.

NOTES

Chapter One:
Understanding Hubert Selby, Jr.

1. John O'Brien, "Interview with Hubert Selby, Jr.," *Review of Contemporary Fiction* 1 (Summer 1981):333.

2. Letter from Hubert Selby, Jr., to James R. Giles, April 16, 1996.

3. Langenheim, Bill, "Interview with Hubert Selby, Jr.," *Enclitic* 10 (1988):26.

4. Paul Metcalf, "Herman and Hubert: The Odd Couple," *Review of Contemporary Fiction* 1 (Summer 1981):364–69.

5. Langenheim, 14–28.

6. Allan Vorda, "Examining the Disease: An Interview with Hubert Selby, Jr." *Literary Review* 35 (Winter 1992):296.

7. Giles, telephone interview with Selby, March 31, 1996.

8. This biographical information is from *Contemporary Authors,* ed. Clare D. Kinsman, vols. 13–16, Detroit: Cole, 1965, 1966, 1975, p. 715; and from Giles's March 31, 1996, telephone interview with Selby.

9. Langenheim.

10. In large part because Selby's reputation has from the beginning been that of an "underground writer" and because he is apparently one of the most determinedly private of literary figures, much about these early years of his life remains vague.

11. Letter, Selby-Giles, April 14, 1996.

12. S. E. Gontarski, "Last Exit to Brooklyn: An Interview with Hubert Selby," *Review of Contemporary Fiction* 10 (Fall 1990):111.

Chapter Two:
Last Exit to Brooklyn

1. Josephine Hendin, *Vulnerable People: A View of American Fiction since 1945* (Oxford: Oxford University Press, 1978), p. 59.

2. Joseph X. Brennan, "Ironic and Symbolic Structure in Crane's *Maggie*," *Maggie: A Girl of the Streets,* ed. Thomas A. Gullason (New York: Norton, 1979), pp. 183–84.

3. For a more complete discussion of the absurdist existentialism that dominates *Last Exit to Brooklyn,* see Giles, *The Naturalistic Inner-City Novel in America: Encounters with the Fat Man* (Columbia, S.C.: University of South Carolina Press, 1995).

4. Gerd Hurm, *Fragmented Urban Images: The American City in Modern Fiction from Stephen Crane to Thomas Pynchon* (New York: Peter Lang, 1991), p. 274.

5. Tony Tanner, *City of Words: American Fiction 1950– 1970* (New York: Harper & Row, 1971), pp. 344–45.

6. Joyce Carol Oates, "The Nightmare of Naturalism: Harriette Arnow's *The Dollmaker*," *New Heaven, New Earth: The Visionary Experience in Literature* (New York: Vanguard, 1974), p. 110.

7. Vorda, 290.

8. Charles D. Peavy, "Hubert Selby and the Tradition of Moral Satire," *Satire Newsletter* 6 (Spring 1969):37.

9. Selby states that his "literary idol is Isaac Babel" and that "he believes that his only influence is Beethoven" (*Contemporary Authors,* vols. 13–16, p. 715). In the March 31, 1996, telephone interview with this writer he reaffirmed his devotion to

these two figures, saying about Babel, "I just love that little guy." He did state though that there have undoubtedly been many other influences on his work, specifically citing Céline as an example.

10. O'Brien, "Interview," 333.

11. Langenheim, 22.

12. Hubert Selby, Jr., *Last Exit to Brooklyn* (New York: Grove, 1964), p. 23.

13. For what still remains the best single discussion of this aspect of the Maggie characterization, see Donald Pizer's "Stephen Crane's *Maggie* and American Naturalism," *Criticism* 7 (Spring 1965):168–75.

14. Stephen Crane, "Maggie: A Girl of the Streets," The University of Virginia Edition of *The Works of Stephen Crane*, I (Bowery Tales), ed. Fredson Bowers (Charlottesville: University Press of Virginia, 1969), p. 27.

15. Richard Gehr, "Last Exit to Brooklyn," *American Film* 15 (May 1990):34–39, 48.

16. Richard A. Wertime, "Psychic Vengeance in *Last Exit to Brooklyn*," *Literature and Psychology* 24 (4 November 1974):154.

17. Charles D. Peavy, "The Sin of Pride and Selby's *Last Exit to Brooklyn*," *Critique* 3, iii (1969):35.

18. Gilbert Sorrentino, "Addenda 1981: After *Last Exit to Brooklyn*," *Review of Contemporary Fiction* 1 (Summer 1981):348.

Chapter Three: *The Room*

1. Hubert Selby, Jr., *The Room* (New York: Grove, 1971), pp. 99–100.

2. Jerome Klinkowitz, "Fiction: The 1960s to the Present,"

in *American Literary Scholarship: An Annual 1992,* ed. David J. Nordloh (Durham: Duke University Press, 1994):289.

3. Langenheim, 26–27.

4. Vorda, 296–97.

5. Michael Stephens, for instance, compares *The Room* to Poe's "The Pit and the Pendulum." Stephens, "Hubert Selby, Jr.: The Poet of Prose Masters," *Review of Contemporary Fiction* 1 (Summer 1981):393–94.

6. O'Brien, "Interview," 321–22.

7. Stephens, 393.

8. Josephine Hendin, *Vulnerable People: A View of American Fiction since 1945.* (Oxford: Oxford University Press, 1978), p. 59.

9. John O'Brien provides an extensive analysis of the contrasting "styles" employed in *The Room* in "The Materials of Art in Hubert Selby," *Review of Contemporary Fiction* 1 (Summer 1981):376–79.

10. Eric Mottram, "Free Like the Rest of Us: Violation and Despair in Hubert Selby's Novels," *Review of Contemporary Fiction* 1 (Summer 1981):344.

Chapter Four: *The Demon*

1. Dean Flower, Review of Selby's *The Demon* in *The New York Times Book Review* (November 14, 1976):69.

2. Paul D. Zimmerman, "Wild about Harry," *Newsweek* 88 (November 1, 1976):85,87.

3. Hubert Selby, Jr., *The Demon* (Chicago: Playboy Press, 1976), p. 3.

4. O'Brien, "Interview," 321.

5. For a discussion of this kind of naturalism as it appears in works by Michael Gold, Richard Wright, Nelson Algren, John Rechy, and Joyce Carol Oates as well as in *Last Exit to Brooklyn,* see Giles, *The Naturalistic Inner-City Novel in America.*

6. Paul Metcalf's "Herman and Hubert: The Odd Couple" is an extensive comparison of Selby and Herman Melville as "moral" novelists. Metcalf, 364–69.

7. Sorrentino, 347.

8. Langenheim, 14–28.

Chapter Five:
Requiem for a Dream

1. Metcalf, 368.

2. Vorda, 301.

3. O'Brien, "Interview," 322.

4. Kenneth John Atchity, "Hubert Selby's *Requiem for a Dream:* A Primer of Vision," *Review of Contemporary Fiction* 1 (Summer 1981):404.

5. Sorrentino, 348.

6. Hubert Selby, Jr., *Requiem for a Dream* (Chicago: Playboy Press, 1978), p. 9.

7. Norman Mailer, *The Armies of the Night* (New American Library, 1968), p. 320.

8. Kenneth Tindall, "The Fishing at Coney Island: Hubert Selby Jr. and the Cult of Authenticity," *Review of Contemporary Fiction* 1 (Summer 1981):370.

Chapter Six:
Song of the Silent Snow

1. Hubert Selby, Jr., *Song of the Silent Snow and Other Stories* (New York: Grove, 1986), p. 136.

2. Langenheim, 27.

3. In an April 16, 1996, letter Selby offers additional information regarding the collection. He writes that "OF WHALES AND DREAMS was written for Green Peace. They put out a coffee table book: WHALES, A CELEBRATION, and I was asked to contribute something and this story was the result." He then provides the dates for each story in *Song of the Silent Snow:*

"Puberty"—1957, rev. 1981
"Hi Champ"—1978
"Fortune Cookie"—1978
"Liebesnacht"—1981
"The Coat"—1978
"The Musician"—1979
"The Sound"—1967
"A Penny for Your Thoughts"—1958
"A Little Respect"—1978
"Fat Phils Day"—1957
"Indian Summer"—1957
"Song of the Silent Snow"—1981
"Im Being Good"—1980
"Double Feature"—1957
"Of Whales and Dreams"—1980.

4. Vorda, 296.

BIBLIOGRAPHY

Works by
Hubert Selby, Jr.

Novels

Last Exit to Brooklyn. New York: Grove, 1964; London: Calder & Boyars, 1968.

The Room. New York: Grove, 1971; London: Calder & Boyars, 1972.

The Demon. New York: Playboy Press, 1976.

Requiem for a Dream. New York: Playboy Press, 1978.

Short-Story Collection

Song of the Silent Snow. New York and London: Marion Boyars, 1986; reprinted as *Song of the Silent Snow and Other Stories.* New York: Grove, 1987.

Other

"And Baby Makes Three" and "Loves Labors Lost." *New American Story,* ed. Donald M. Allen and Robert Creeley. New York: Grove, 1965.

Periodical Publications

"Another Day Another Dollar." *New Directions* 17 (1961):215–24.

"The Birthday Boy." *Enclitic* 10, i (1988):9–12.

BIBLIOGRAPHY

"Double Feature," *Neon* 4 (1959):50–59.

"Fat Phils Day." *Evergreen Review* 11 (August 1967):52–53.

"Happy Birthday." *Evergreen Review* 13 (August 1969):35–37.

"Home for Christmas." *Neon* 2 (1956):22–25.

"Loves/ Labours/ Lost." *Black Mountain Review* 3 (Autumn 1957):169–86.

Review of *Lament,* by David Carson. *Village Voice,* 1 November 1973, p. 28.

"Solving the Ice-Cream Cone Problem." *Evergreen Review* 12 (August 1968):57–58.

"Tralala." *Provincetown Review* 3 (1960):73+.

"The Queen Is Dead." *Evergreen Review* 8 (December 1964): 13–17, 93.

Interviews

Gontarski, S. E. "Last Exit to Brooklyn: An Interview with Hubert Selby." *Review of Contemporary Fiction* 10 (Fall 1990):111–15.

Langenheim, Bill. "Interview with Hubert Selby, Jr." *Enclitic* 10, i (1988):14–28.

O'Brien, John. "Interview with Hubert Selby, Jr." *Review of Contemporary Fiction* 1 (Summer 1981):315–35.

Vorda, Allan. "Examining the Disease: An Interview with Hubert Selby, Jr." *Literary Review* 35 (Winter 1992):288–302.

BIBLIOGRAPHY

Critical Works about Selby

Articles and Sections of Books

Atchity, Kenneth John. "Hubert Selby's *Requiem for a Dream:* A Primer of Vision." *Review of Contemporary Fiction* 1 (Summer 1981):399–405. Interprets Selby's fourth novel from a perspective of the failure of "vision," stating that the visions of "light" and "life" shared by its central characters are perverted and crushed by "the darkness inside themselves and inside our society."

Binet, Roland. "The Mirror of Man." *Review of Contemporary Fiction* 1 (Summer 1981):380–88. Certainly one of the most perceptive essays on Selby, it discusses his fiction as a study of characters controlled by both external totalitarianism (social determinism) and internal totalitarianism ("instincts, greed, lust, jealousy, perversions").

Buckeye, Robert. "Some Preliminary Notes towards a Study of Selby." *Review of Contemporary Fiction* 1 (Summer 1981):374–75. A brief discussion of the style and narrative perspective that are unique to Selby's fiction.

Byrne, Jack. "Selby's Yahoos: The Brooklyn Breed, A Dialogue of the Mind with Itself." *Review of Contemporary Fiction* 1 (Summer 1981):349–53. An interview-essay with Byrne in which he compares the characters in Selby's fiction with William Shakespeare's Caliban and Jonathan Swift's Yahoos: "Shakespeare gave us the prototype, Swift gave us the tribe, and Selby documented their presence among us."

BIBLIOGRAPHY

Gehr, Richard. "Last Exit to Brooklyn." *American Film* 15 (May 1990):34–39, 48. A discussion of the 1989 filming of *Last Exit to Brooklyn* in the Red Hook neighborhood of Brooklyn, it contains some brief but extremely perceptive analysis of the novel and provides information about Selby's involvement in, and enthusiasm for, director Uli Edel's film.

Giles, James R. "The Game of Mum as Theme and Narrative Technique in Hubert Selby's *Last Exit to Brooklyn*." In his *The Naturalistic Inner-City Novel in America: Encounters with the Fat Man*. 119–38. Columbia, S.C.: University of South Carolina Press, 1995. Discusses *Last Exit to Brooklyn* as a work of "absurdist naturalism."

Hendin, Josephine. "Angries: S-M as a Literary Style." In her *Vulnerable People: A View of American Fiction since 1945*. 53–71. Oxford: Oxford University Press, 1978. Describes Selby as "a clinician of male violence . . . whose novels have the immediacy of primitive art."

Howard, June. "Documents, Dramas, and Discontinuities: The Narrative Strategies of American Naturalism." In her *Form and History in American Literary Naturalism*. 142–82. Chapel Hill: University of North Carolina Press, 1985. Briefly but perceptively argues that *Last Exit to Brooklyn* be considered a work of "latter-day naturalism not only because of its pessimism but because it does indeed have crucial structural similarities to naturalist novels of an earlier period."

Hurm, Gerd. "Hubert Selby: *Last Exit to Brooklyn*." In his *Fragmented Urban Images: The American City in Modern Fiction from Stephen Crane to Thomas Pynchon*. New York: Peter Lang, 1991. 273–99. Extremely valuable essay relating

BIBLIOGRAPHY

Last Exit to Brooklyn to both the naturalist and modernist traditions in American fiction focusing upon the city.

Kermode, Frank. "'Obscenity' and the 'Public Interest.'" *New American Review* 3 (April 1968):229–44. Account of the 1967 London, England, obscenity trial of *Last Exit to Brooklyn*.

Lane, James B. "Violence and Sex in the Post-War Popular Urban Novel: With a Consideration of Harold Robbins's *A Stone for Danny Fisher* and Hubert Selby, Jr.'s *Last Exit to Brooklyn*." *Journal of Popular Culture* 8 (Fall 1974):295–308. Calls Selby a "moralist" whose "use of sex was unromantic" and argues that he, unlike Robbins, grew as an artist after the publication of his first novel.

Lewis, Harry. "Some Things I Want to Say about Hubert Selby's Work." *Review of Contemporary Fiction* 1 (Summer 1981):413–15. Brief discussion of Selby as a "storyteller."

Metcalf, Paul. "Herman and Hubert: The Odd Couple." *Review of Contemporary Fiction* 1 (Summer 1981):364–69. Compares Selby's work to that of Herman Melville and condemns *The Demon* and *Requiem for a Dream* as representing a turn by Selby to the "commercial."

Mottram, Eric. "Free Like the Rest of Us: Violation and Despair in Hubert Selby's Novels." *Review of Contemporary Fiction,* 1 (Summer 1981):353–63. One of the best pieces of criticism on Selby, it describes his novels as "a massive text enquiring into the nature of violation and the law" in contemporary society. Also relates Selby's work to the rebellious writing of the 1960s.

Oates, Joyce Carol. "The Nightmare of Naturalism: Harriette

BIBLIOGRAPHY

Arnow's *The Dollmaker.*" In her *New Heaven, New Earth: The Visionary Experience in Literature.* New York: Vanguard, 1974. 99–110. Compares *Last Exit to Brooklyn* unfavorably to Arnow's novel by asserting that Selby's novel "is totally absorbed in an analysis of bodily existence" and thus denies its characters a "spiritual" nature.

O'Brien, John. "The Materials of Art in Hubert Selby." *Review of Contemporary Fiction* 1 (Summer 1981):376–79. Perceptive analysis of Selby's narrative style, focusing especially on his use of a "scale" of four "styles" in *The Room.*

Oppenheimer, Joel. "Memories." *Review of Contemporary Fiction* 1 (Summer 1981):397–98. Brief reminiscence of the author's friendship and experiences with Selby in Brooklyn.

Peavy, Charles D. "Hubert Selby and the Tradition of Moral Satire." *Satire Newsletter* 6 (Spring 1969):35–39. A perceptive essay that discusses Selby as a "religious-moralist-satirist" in the tradition of Swift and Alexander Pope and the artists William Hogarth and Hieronymus Bosch.

———. "The Sin of Pride and Selby's *Last Exit to Brooklyn.*" *Critique* 11, iii (1969):35–42. Still one of the best discussions of Selby's first novel, it argues that "Selby has an almost obsessive concern with sin" and that the characters in the novel are dominated by "arrogant" and/or "self-destructive . . . pride."

Singer, Robert. "Only the Dead: Urban Milieu in the Contemporary Naturalist Film," *Excavatio* forthcoming 1997. Contains perceptive discussion of film version of *Last Exit to Brooklyn.*

BIBLIOGRAPHY

Sorrentino, Gilbert. "Addenda 1981: After *Last Exit to Brooklyn.*" *Review of Contemporary Fiction* 1 (Summer 1981):346–48. An addition to his earlier essay "The Art of Hubert Selby," it treats *The Room, The Demon,* and *Requiem for a Dream* and praises Selby for having created a lasting art out of subject matter and language that had previously been assumed to be inappropriate for meaningful literature.

————. "The Art of Hubert Selby." *Kulchur* 13 (Spring 1964):27–43. The first extensive discussion of Selby's work, written by one of his closest friends, it offers valuable insight into the degree to which environment severely restricts the lives of the characters in *Last Exit to Brooklyn* and praises Selby as "a finished artist" and "a meticulous student of the lower-class, the underworld, the dispossessed."

Stephens, Michael. "Hubert Selby, Jr.: The Poet of Prose Masters." *Review of Contemporary Fiction* 1 (Summer 1981):389–97. Praises Selby's poetic sensibility, arguing that *Last Exit to Brooklyn* "annihilated naturalism and gave poetry to fiction."

Tanner, Tony. "On the Parapet." In his *City of Words: American Fiction 1950–1970.* New York: Harper & Row, 1971. 344–71. In this chapter devoted primarily to the fiction of Norman Mailer, Tanner briefly discusses *Last Exit to Brooklyn* as a study of a human "behavioral sink" and criticizes Selby's novel as being overly "demoralizing."

Tindall, Kenneth. "The Fishing at Coney Island: Hubert Selby, Jr. and the Cult of Authenticity." *Review of Contemporary Fiction* 1 (Summer 1981):370–3. Brief, impressionistic study of the language and the trope of drug addiction in *Requiem for a Dream.*

BIBLIOGRAPHY

Wertime, Richard A. "Psychic Vengeance in *Last Exit to Brooklyn.*" *Literature and Psychology* 24 (4 November 1974):153–66. A vital early investigation of the psychological dimensions of *Last Exit,* it stands as a seminal exploration of this aspect of Selby's fiction.

————. "On the Question of Style in Hubert Selby, Jr.'s Fiction." *Review of Contemporary Fiction* 1 (Summer 1981):406–13. Describes Selby as "a doubly threatening writer" because he deals with "material that is socially taboo" and "commits stylistic violence upon his reader" by failing to observe "the most revered criteria of control."

INDEX

INDEX

INDEX

INDEX

INDEX

INDEX

INDEX